DETAILS

DE-
TAILS

A Stylist's Secrets to Creating Inspired Interiors

Lili Diallo
Text written with Zoë Wolff

*Principal photography
by Annie Schlechter*

Clarkson Potter/Publishers
New York

Copyright © 2010 by Lili Diallo

Published in the United States by Clarkson Potter/Publishers, an
imprint of the Crown Publishing Group, a division of Random House,
Inc., New York.
www.crownpublishing.com
www.clarksonpotter.com

CLARKSON POTTER is a trademark and POTTER with colophon
is a registered trademark of Random House, Inc.

Library of Congress Cataloging-in-Publication Data
Diallo, Lili.
   Details: a stylist's secrets to creating inspired interiors / Lili Diallo.
—1st ed.
       p.   cm
   Includes index.
1. Interior decoration accessories.   I. Title.
NK2115.5.A25   D53   2010
747—dc22   2009049733

ISBN 978-0-307-59151-7

Printed in China

Design by VSA Partners, Inc., New York

Photographs by Annie Schlechter except those by Lili Diallo on
pages 126 (top), 164, 166, 168, 169, 170, 171, 172, 173, 229
(bottom), 231, and 233; those by Lili Diallo with Jada Vogt on pages
56, 58, 59, 60, 61, 62, 63, 64, 65, 66, 67, 190, 192, 194, 195,
196, 197, 198, 199, 200, 201, 202, 203, 216, 219, 220, 221, 222,
223, 224, and 225; and those by Lesley Unruh on pages 228, 229
(top), 230, 232, 234, 235, 236, 238, 240, 241, 242, and 243.

10 9 8 7 6 5 4 3 2 1

First Edition

To all the stylists in the making,
my wish is that this book will inspire
you and...bliss you out!

CON-TENTS

8 INSPIRATION
   Fais Comme Chez Toi…
   (Or, Make Yourself at Home)

15 Chez Moi

31 TEXTURE
35 The Modernist Barn
45 Dorothy Draper, Meet French Glamour
57 Ode to Scandinavian Simplicity
69 New Traditionalism in a Glass Box

79 COLOR
83 A Vision in White
95 Staging a Bright Intervention
107 The Neutral-Thread Formula
117 An Apartment Fellini Would Love

129 OBJECTS
133 Black, White, and Goth All Over
143 Arte Povera Bliss
153 A Midcentury Cottage with Storytelling Soul
165 A Poetic Stance in Paris

175 MOOD
179 The Ice Storm
191 The Multicultural Loft Odyssey
205 An English Garden in a Tiny Penthouse
217 Cinema Verité in an Alcove Studio

226 DASH OF STYLE
249 Acknowledgments
250 Where to Find It
253 Index

FAIS COMME CHEZ TOI...

(or, make yourself at home)

THE HOMES MAGAZINE FOR MODERN LIVING   livingetc.com

VOGUE®

VOGUE . N° 898 . JUIN-

VOGUE®

APRIL 2007

ELLE

JANVIER 2008 *Vogue / Les Publications Condé Nast S.A. / WWW.VOGUE.COM*

AUSTRALIAN SUMMER 2006

Anything can be an inspiration, from the Day-Glo T-shirt of an angst-ridden teen on the subway to the obscure and gorgeous museum housed in a small *hôtel particulier* (the Parisian version of a town house) in the Marais in Paris.

Books, art, movies, people, nature—all are part of the algorithm. I can be on vacation on the Basque coast in France or on Nantucket Island having breakfast overlooking the ocean, and the color nuances of that moment will lead to a bathroom palette.

I was a total bookworm during my early teenage years, and a lit major in college. In my Dostoyevsky phase, I remember feeling completely transported into the Russian nineteenth-century bourgeois homes of *The Idiot,* where a samovar always seems to be at hand and the tortured soul of beautiful Nastasya Filipovna was forever "on the verge." Then it was the decadent salon of the Guermantes in the Proust saga; later, the Villa Malapatre's near-empty rooms in Godard's film *Le Mépris.* I wanted to live in all these improbable places, and while I was reading or watching, I could. Literature and paintings were like my blue period, film and fashion my white and gray period, and my trip to India my pink and red period.

I think of all this when I am in need of inspiration. I remember seeing a lady in India wearing a gorgeous pink silk sari with a navy-blue choli. I was entranced. The lively pink paired with austere navy was a complete revelation. It makes me think of that Diana Vreeland quote: "Pink [is] the navy blue of India." I see pink as a life-force color now. It appears throughout my home—in a pouf in my office, in the poster in my bedroom. When I feel I need to quicken the pulse of a room, I almost always reach for pink.

From a young age, I've also had a compulsion to make rooms more beautiful. No matter where I went, I would find myself mentally redecorating the place. (My sister thought I was crazy and blamed my Cancer-rising, Libra-moon Virgo sun sign for it!)

And while I love reading, writing is my bête noire. It is more natural for me to express narratives visually, through home or still-life styling. It fills me with joy to bring rooms to their full potential and to help uncover untold stories and hidden beauty.

By showcasing my loft to kick off this book, I want to offer a peek inside the stylist's mind. It's very different from that of a decorator. I don't read blueprints, don't have a complete decorating scheme. It's more of an organic process for me. Stylists dig in to what we see around us, what made our heart beat faster while we were viewing an exhibit, what lingered from a Sunday jog along the river. In decoration, a room might call for a certain wallpaper, whereas if I like a wallpaper pattern, I try to make it work because I've already built a story and a room around it.

When I walk into a home that I am styling for a photo shoot, I fix any immediate spatial issues (such as furniture in the wrong place) first. I dig up the owner's story by finding out about their travel memories, favorite paintings, beloved films. This kind of one-on-one anthropology serves to uncover a client's style and give it a name, a flavor, a voice. The stylist's task is to put the puzzle together. I come up with a color or a style for the character, again drawing references from things that have inspired me. The heavy blue silk drapes of Ingres's *Odalisque* antechamber could trigger the blue of a bedroom wall. Richard Gere's apartment in *American Gigolo* might evoke a clamoring touch in a living room. I love how creativity, individuality, and psyche found a voice in the grander scheme of decoration in the homes in this book. For example, the house of Michella Martello and Mauro Bareti acquired a strong narrative through found objects and travelers' bounty. The complete antipode is Tom Delavan's apartment. Sitting on a cloud of blue-gray dreams, it seems to have found its voice in some more ephemeral region of the mind. There is no such thing as "wrong" taste or styling, as long as it comes from an authentic place and is ultimately portrayed with confidence. I believe everyone has a stylist within. This book will help you unlock yours.

Chez Moi

With its view of the Manhattan skyline, the East River, and the Manhattan
Bridge, my home is my haven, a place where I can stare out at the big
city while simultaneously feeling I'm in my own world. I moved into this loft

in DUMBO more than six years ago. When
I first saw it, I thought: too industrial, too
raw, too ugly, and…I wanted a garden.
There were brick walls painted yellow in
the main area and orange in what is now

my office—all against an olive-green concrete floor! Transforming the
space to my liking seemed too daunting. But after much deliberation,
I took the leap. I figured it was conveniently located and that I could use
the 2,000 square feet both as a styling lab and for prop storage.

When I moved in, I painted the walls and floor of the office white.
I wanted to have at least one room where I could retreat. My idea was to
redo the house bit by bit as I was living there. In a big space, mistakes
can be costly and emotionally draining. About a year later, I decided to
paint the rest of the place all white but keep the green floor everywhere
besides the office. The loft has so many textures and odd features that
bright white makes it look pulled together and clean. My former apartment
was much smaller, and whatever furniture I had seemed floating and
lonely in the big loft so I started to search for more pieces. The decoration
evolved organically as I got to know my apartment better. I have always
approached spaces thinking about objects, mood, and color, and working
at *Domino* taught me to pay equal attention to texture and scale—both
major factors in crafting a beautiful interior.

Personalizing the Home Office

Triage was needed here! I immediately painted the orange brick walls and green floor in Decorator's White from Benjamin Moore. Then the room felt a bit sterile, so I painted the door red. Ikea Lack shelves hold various objects that make me happy and that I sometimes use for my shoots. The shelving unit below was there when I moved in, and I painted it white.

I style by varying height and textures while maintaining a simple color scheme. I always love the way oversized books look when stacked—dynamic and artsy.

My little desk—a kitchen table that was green before I coated it in a light Benjamin Moore gray—is elevated by the Selene chair by industrial design genius Vico Magistretti, which first appeared in 1969 and was recently reissued by the Italian furniture company Heller. I can't get enough of its simplicity and modern elegance—all in molded plastic. The pouf hails from the souk of Marrakech and relates to the door hue without mirroring it.

Creating a Story for Your Home

This inspiration tableau is an encouragement to gather up your favorite things and see what narrative unfolds. You can fashion your home around a color palette, textures, the whimsical details of a thermos's cherry-blossom branch. The smoky blues and grays could be translated into upholstery, the chrome could be the base of a sofa, the white could be applied to the walls, and the wood could suggest a dining table or your existing floors. An inspiration tableau can clarify your taste and make decision-making smoother.

Just a Red Panel

Contrary to popular belief, white is not the small-space panacea. I find it can be sad and dorm room–like. For my tiny bedroom, I wanted a color that was enveloping but not dark. I decided to paint just one wall in Ralph Lauren's Mai Tai. Having color on a single panel kept my room more open and undone—just how I like it. The red hue makes the space feel intimate at night and happy in the morning light.

The headboard, originally created for a *Domino* shoot, is re-covered in a Brunschwig & Fils toile de Jouy. I love the French eighteenth-century allusion against the red wall and the white bricks. The Ikea cabinet and the For Like Ever poster, designed by an art director and upgraded with a glossy gray frame, contribute some pop energy. The chest is by interior designer Celerie Kemble for Laneventure. High/low, antique/modern, bright/subdued—to me, a successful home is heterogeneous in style but still cohesive, whether through a color palette or some other unifying scheme.

The Poetry of Ordinary Things

Repurposing involves seeing things not for what they are, but for what they could be. A small glass jam jar or an empty cosmetic bottle can become a cool vase.

En Vogue

My dining area is a very loose take on a *Vogue* image of Plum Sykes's dining room. I didn't want to copy it verbatim, but I loved that English garden teatime vibe. For me, inspiration is seeing something you like and filtering it through your own sensibility and circumstances. That is what gives a space authorship.

When something in a room seems off, I try to look at it from a new angle and adapt the décor to it. I embrace happy accidents. They are very often what gives a home its strongest style statements. At first glance, a chintz room divider is not at all appropriate for my industrial loft. But after living with it placed behind my dining table— with every intention of re-covering it in subdued gray linen—I grew to love its offbeat charm.

Screen Switch

As a restless experimenter, I decided to see what would happen if I styled my dining area in a totally different way. Changing only two key elements can lead to a completely altered room. This arty cheetah-print-covered screen, devised with my friend Tori Jones (see her apartment on pages 68–77 in the Texture chapter) for a *Domino* shoot, is a wink to YSL's safari collection of the 1970s, which I have always adored. I paired the screen with a Parsons white lacquer table that I had bought as a desk for my office. Everything else in the dining area remains the same, but the overall look is more fashion-world sleek, which suits my mood du jour.

Stylist's Secrets:

Selecting a Screen
Versatile, easily changeable, and timeless, screens are great add-ons for rooms. Choose the height and texture depending on how you wish to use the screen:

* Elegantly tall and thin to dress up or hide a tiny dysfunctional corner

* Wide and low as a room partition that still allows light to flow through the top

* Wide and tall as a background or theatrical movable décor

* Upholstered in fabric to warm the space

* In lacquered wood to add a chic edge

Cheap Trick

Most people leap to the conclusion that a well-worn or no-longer-beloved sofa must go. I am a huge advocate of re-covering. You can buy your own gorgeous piece of fabric or unearth a vintage linen tablecloth and toss it over your sofa. Then, if you decice you love that fabric, you can call in your upholsterer to affix it permanently. When I saw this linen at B&J Fabrics in New York City, I got so inspired. It absolutely elevates my Ikea sofa hiding underneath. The plaid navy linen with gold threads combines with the wood cabinet and the deer art for a cheeky urban take on a Highlands lodge. The old-fashioned roses, the portrait of a young man in a gold frame, and the image of Charlotte Gainsbourg in bed chime in with a romantic-punk riff. I bought four yards of fabric and definitely plan to make it permanent.

Sun King Grandeur and Refined Eclecticism

The French fascination with *folie,* or a tinge of mad extravagance, dates further back than Louis XVI. (Granted, the neoclassical faux farm he built on the grounds of Versailles where Marie Antoinette could milk real cows ranks as maddest *of all*!) But how does one successfully infuse an interior with a dash of humor without becoming a laughingstock? My first rule of thumb is not to try too hard. True *folie* comes only when *you* see nothing out of the ordinary about it: These humorous details convey a sense of playfulness, and can be swapped out as easily as they were swapped in. Above, the Marie Antoinette–worthy tassels complement my eighteenth-century French bergère chair and make me forget the cheap doorknob that I never got around to changing. Opposite, it's all about weaving a thread of color and humor through an eclectic mix.

A Narrative Approach

I fell in love with this Danish midcentury leather sofa at the store, but once I got it home, all I could think was, What on earth do I do with rust? So I decided to paint the wall behind it aqua blue to bring out the sofa's warm tones. The extra *loooooong* hot pink linen pillow stretched across the seat distracts from the sobriety of that rust color.

Hanging art can be really tricky and nerve-wracking. Most artworks are mounted too high or too low, unfortunately placed (e.g., a tiny framed painting looking lost and lonely on a giant wall), or curated within an inch of their lives. Then there is the ubiquitous gallery-style approach, which has a more organized grid, repetition of frames, and equal spacing. My take? Mix. It. Up. Hanging pictures is a poetic exercise for me; my approach is salon style, which is more organic.

On my office wall, I didn't want to drill big holes in the brick; so I used the nails that had been hammered into the walls by previous renters and created a flow around them.

Stylist's Secrets:

Effortless Art Display

* Hang works of art as you find them, creating an organic cluster. Choose one piece as a focal point and build a narrative around it.

* Measuring equal distance between frames can help create a perfect balance even in a salon-style hanging.

* As when creating any collection, framing your artwork in the same style or color creates a more cohesive, tailored look.

* Too many small frames will look messy and random. Four or five should be the limit.

* Go for a touch of gold in a sea of black, or mix white modern minimalist frames with eighteenth-century paintings for a pedigree twist.

* Don't be afraid to display art on the floor for a more casual, artsy look.

TEX-TURE

Texture is an essential part of decorating. It gives a place soul. Texture is more than just a tactile sensation. It's a visual and visceral experience. As a stylist, I think of it in terms of a feeling or specific moments. If I want to re-create a weekend in the country, I take woodsy elements, whether a farmhouse table or a drawing of a tree, to hark back to that bucolic experience. To conjure a salon depicted in a painting I love, a velvet-covered armchair might do the trick.

If you don't want to endure major architectural changes or a whole paint job, there are plenty of quick, affordable tricks to add texture.

It can be achieved through a mélange of textiles, through color, by mixing furniture from different time periods, or by hanging art with frames of varying materials. It can be a simple flourish like a hot pink linen pillow strewn across a leather sofa, a pleated silk pendant lamp crowning a wooden dining table, a cluster of family photographs hung whimsically on a wall. And last, varying patterns create a visual dynamic, which could beautifully translate as texture. Ultimately, texturing results from layering and unexpected clashes that convey a living, breathing energy to a space, and that can give the illusion of architecture when there is none, personality to a place devoid of it, energy when a home has gone to sleep.

I grew up in old houses with a mix of antiques, well-worn furniture, and a lot of Asian statuettes and knickknacks. Modernity was not part of my childhood vernacular. At that time, antique furniture equaled grandma style to me; however, I did love living in an old house and found it cozy and comforting. I found my best friend's modern apartment a bit depressing and a little sterile, so I used to think it was a "poor" home, even though I realized later it was quite the opposite. I remember thinking, Why don't they have some old kilims? At the same time, I would come home and wonder, Why don't we have something fun and lacquered? I am always pulled between these two poles. To this day, I feel something is missing in one-note homes. In my own home and in my styling work, I strive to make old and new collide, to bravely juxtapose fabrics and eras, to visually intuit what will give a place texture and soul.

Plastic is a like a decorating wink in a room. The Philippe Starck stool is a humorous touch that keeps this corner from reading as too austere.

The Modernist Barn

The house Rosemary Hallgarten shares with her husband and two sons is a temple to rich minimalism that mirrors the aesthetic of her craftwork. Originally an old barn, the converted rustic-modern home totals 9,000

square feet. Eager to keep the essence of the barn (structure, wood floors, and paneling), the family limited new features to the windows and an addition for the kitchen, offices, and Rosemary's studio. Through a symphony of wood and metal architecture, wool and leather furniture, and warm textiles, Rosemary fills and humanizes the vast space.

Rosemary is a rug designer and an ultimate texture connoisseur. She is constantly experimenting with new visual and tactile combinations. Her rugs are traditionally crafted in South America and Asia, but the patterns and palettes belie her distinctly modernist sensibilities. Her mother also designed rugs and collaborated with many celebrated artists of her time. Rosemary clearly inherited her mother's glamorous bohemian ways, as well as the impeccably tailored manner of her English father. Her house shows how texture can be the starting point of a home, not the final flourishes. The dark wood from the old barn dictated the interior textural scheme, which Rosemary balanced with clean modern furniture. All it took to boost the coziness factor was playing around with her existing throws, objects, and accessories.

Blending Styles

Wood meets metal; tradition meets modern architecture: What was a former barn (there was also a pigsty, which has been torn down) has been reinterpreted as a contemporary-rustic oasis.

Brushstrokes

Metal, wood, and stone is a chic trio that could easily inspire a great indoor scheme. The rust peeking through the seal on the silo looks like Julian Schnabel brushstrokes.

The Rug Archive

Rosemary's office is a little like the souk of Marrakech. It's where she archives samples of every single rug she has ever designed. I'm amazed at how stacked textiles on basic steel shelves impart such presence. It's almost debauched how luxurious it looks! Interspersing textiles you've collected with books and objects has a layered elegance worthy of *The World of Interiors.*

Texturing with Frames

Few things personalize a home more than family photographs. Rosemary's mostly black-and-white pictures are framed almost exclusively in metals of different finishes (shiny, matte, hammered), making the collection elegantly unified but not too same-same. Clustering the frames in tight groups makes the scene more intimate. Antique Etruscan pottery that Rosemary brought back from a trip to Beirut intersperses another nostalgic sentiment.

Minimal and Tribal

A primitive metal pot from Portobello Market in London brings this area into focus, tying in the metal moments surrounding the fireplace and creating a narrative with the art on the wall. (The Spartan art choices are generally subdued and blend in naturally with the house's natural textures.) Most classic twentieth- and twenty-first-century modern furniture is mass-produced these days, so in minimalist homes with that sort of furniture, it's important to pay extra attention to handcrafted and historical elements that add depth and humanity.

Dark Wood Modernity

Rosemary's furniture selection is a paean to great modern design, with sofas by Philippe Starck and de Sede in earthy leather and wool emphasizing clean lines and a controlled palette.

Minimalism is one of the hardest things to get right in an interior. To offset sterility, visual texture becomes crucial. It's like the *"nouveau roman"* of interiors; an attention to detail will make the story. The singular pop of the rug (with a thick pile that feels like butter under your feet!) is the room's happy pill, and a way to define a homey hangout zone. Low-slung couches look sexy in grand rooms. A rug over the back of a sofa and a few blankets cozy things up.

A Grand Entrance

The silo encases a modern circular staircase with classic proportions that leads to the upper floor, containing the offices, the bedrooms, and the bathrooms. Taking her cue from the original dark floor, Rosemary replaced the wood with slate-gray concrete—more practical for the foyer and also environmentally friendly—that bears a design based on her round "Twig" rug. I pulled this chair down from Rosemary's office to make the area more welcoming but still elegant and grand. I like how its high back loosely repeats the banister bars, accentuating the curve of the staircase. I also placed the antique Etruscan pottery directly on the floor to extend the notion of effortless warmth.

Side Table Dialogue

In the corner of the living room, a midcentury Knoll side table stands out against the wood. The zebra-motif cushion is the very first cushion Rosemary designed. I styled this vignette to represent the essence of her house. It can be emulated anywhere. The formula: a little modern, a little wood, with any combination of textiles and artwork stacked on the floor, keeping the color palette simple, mostly neutrals with an occasional pop of color. *Et voilà!* A short story that's not too overwrought.

Dorothy Draper, Meet French Glamour

My good friend Lauren is a fashion editor and stylist. She was the fashion director at *Domino,* masterminding stories about the homes of fashion designers and how to live like you dress. While she honed her decorating

sensibilities at the magazine, she would be the first to admit she lacks confidence when it comes to her own home. I find it hard to believe that about Mademoiselle Lauren, who can totally rock a bold outfit.

Lauren solicited so much advice from friends and colleagues that she lost sight of herself. My job was to get her to trust her instincts and not be afraid to make decisions, or even mistakes.

To be fair, Lauren's apartment is in a 1960s building and resembled a dorm room when she moved in. She says, "When I bought the apartment it looked like Miss Havisham's pied-a-terre. It was dark, dusty, and cluttered." When she approached me to help, she had already made some major structural improvements, like installing French doors to create a light-filled bedroom and built-in bookshelves for a salon feel.

I encouraged her to channel her talent for mixing things up in her wardrobe and use the same technique in her apartment. Her tastes vary wildly—she loves Dorothy Draper and collects funky art. "I wanted the apartment to look like 1970s Paris. I thought I could use the modern, undecorated lines to do something a little louche," she says. She wanted cozy and casual but also a dressed-up feeling. The trick was to express these different sides of her without making the place seem mishmoshy.

Metallic Meets Earthy

Lauren is obsessed with her George Smith sofa, but she knew she needed something metallic to cut the Englishness with that French '70s look. We found the Willy Rizzo coffee table together. It's low and lacquered and has an urban attitude that offsets the sofa's aristocratic air. It also complements the chrome legs of a set of violet chairs, expats from Lauren's last apartment (the only pieces worth saving!), and the chrome side table we found on eBay. We balanced it all with a vegetable-dyed dhurrie to bring back the earthy, ethnic style elements Lauren loves in small touches even in her wardrobe— like her macramé bracelets. These clash (yes, clashing can be good!) with the chrome and emphasize the richness of the textiles.

Stylist's Secrets:

Adding Visual Texture
If your home revolves around subdued neutrals or monochromatic tones, mixing patterns and materials will help you add visual texture.

* Mix and match furniture of varied periods and scales and play with finishes. (Or keep the finishes consistent if you don't want to go too far.)

* Consider adding an out-of-this-world furniture piece such as a glam lacquer coffee table for visual impact.

* Throw in fabulous accents like a metallic silver pillow to break up the monotony of an all-too-creamy couch.

Seeing an Abstract Landscape

We found this Paul McCobb wall cabinet in a thrift store and decided to leave it unfinished—its surface looks like an abstract painting and definitely adds texture to the walls. This slightly lost corner just felt like the perfect place to mount it. I leaned the very cool Radiohead album cover (love the old-school glamour of albums!) above it to play off the rainbow array Lauren has so nicely organized on the bookshelves that are opposite it. The square table beneath prevents the cabinet from feeling too random and floaty. The trio of round mirrors breaks up the boxy feeling of the room and gives it a little whimsy. Sometimes an interior needs insouciance and effortlessness. For example, leaving an artwork on the floor until you can find the right place for it can make a strong statement. In my home, I often just end up keeping it there, and I encourage my clients to do the same.

Crinkled Linen

A lamp and plants contribute some TLC and coziness to this corner. Animal-print storage boxes stand in lieu of a side table, and a quick fix of fresh flowers personalizes the area, as does a favorite photograph propped leisurely on the windowsill. The photo was one of the inspirations for Lauren's place—it's the London apartment of fashion designer Bella Freud, shot for *Domino*. Lauren wanted a wall-to-wall red carpet but ultimately couldn't commit to that much of the color. Wall-to-wall carpeting has a reputation for being gauche, but done right it can be amazing. I think it would have looked absolutely stunning and really warmed up the room. *Tant pis!*

Defining the Space

The bedroom turns the volume way up on Dorothy Draper. Lauren chose a muted paisley print wallpaper to hang behind her bed—an excellent alternative to a headboard. The wall-to-wall carpet was left over from a photo shoot. Lauren wasn't crazy about it, but I liked it instantly because it felt a little off. Sometimes that's exactly what a room needs to make it more compelling. Lauren splurged on these gorgeous floor-length drapes that cleverly create a walk-in closet.

I urged Lauren to ditch her all-white bedding, as it made the room too formal and blah. We chose gray-blue sheets in a gauzy texture that feels sexy and airy for the summer. The girly pink pillows relate nicely to the lilac carpet, while the army-blanket-style quilt roughs things up—so the boudoir doesn't seem overly self-conscious. The slightly industrial feel of the desk lamp prevents the room from looking overly sweet. Keeping all lamps in the apartment black creates a visual thread in a place with many competing styles. The vintage tufted footstool is in line with the Draper influence.

Pink Soothes

The tiles give a luxe feeling to the tiny bathroom. "I have always been obsessed with opalescence, especially in relation to water…I think it's the mermaid in me. I loved the dimension in the tile and its delicate but still modern look," Lauren says. Lauren designed the bathroom early on in her renovations, and as she seemed confident about it, I carried the aesthetic through to the bedroom to create visual cohesion.

Color Gradations

All the credit for styling the bookshelves goes to Lauren. She says, "This arrangement came from a friend, who copied it from a famous bookstore in London. I found it irresistible." I adore how she used the red box in the back as a graphic element. En masse, boxes make a powerful statement—the repetition can be almost Warholian, the result like a mini installation. Lauren displays all her Smythson and Hermès boxes on her bookshelves. I do the same with my Ladurée macaroon boxes.

The color photography is from
Pam's friend Susanna Howe.

Ode to Scandinavian Simplicity

Objects and artworks are clearly the essence of this interior—and the passion of Pam Morris and James Gallagher. First-time homeowners, they moved into this three-bedroom apartment in 2007 from a long and narrow

brownstone apartment. Pam, a freelance prop stylist for cookbooks, magazines, and advertising, was a style editor at *Martha Stewart Living* magazine for more than ten years. Jim is a fine artist, curator, and instructor at Parsons School of Design and the creative director at a marketing firm. At the time of their move, Pam was six months pregnant with their daughter, Lily, and they immediately fell for the 1,600-square-foot apartment with its gracious floor plan. The proximity of a beautiful park sealed the deal.

While the space didn't hold a wealth of architectural detail, it was in good shape, and the couple were happy to choose modern efficiency over molding extravaganza. "We bleached the parquet floors and painted everything white. This was the simplest way to make all our things work together, and it created a clean backdrop for the art we wanted to display," Jim says.

Overall, the apartment exudes a sense of comfortable repose. The color palette consists mainly of white and creamy whites highlighted with warm neutrals. Winsome moments invented by Pam and Jim abound. They happily let me tweak the vignettes to showcase their affinity for objects and their acute eye for the beauty of texture in small details.

Breakfast Club

In the all-white kitchen, a small topiary on a stool by the window, and some loose white amaryllis and a bunch of Dusty Miller plunked into a pitcher embellish the simple and breezy space. Mostly furnished with Ikea pieces (the cabinet and table), the monochromatic kitchen is kept warm and inviting through the presence of mundane things like cookbooks, glasses, and plates seen through the cupboard's glass doors. The small plastic side table and ceiling lamp from Kartell add a futuristic streak that ensures the furniture doesn't feel too homogeneous.

In her mind's eye, Pam's inspiration board includes food memoirs (*My Life in France*) and "also Hockney, Paris, Morandi, Japanese cookbooks and craft books," she enumerates.

The Love of Beautiful Things

Separating one of the sons' bedrooms from the office corner, a bookshelf holds some of Pam's props. A virtuoso of tabletop design, she has styled numerous cookbooks and food shoots. "I love tabletop objects, especially handmade organic shapes and beautiful patinas. And I love textiles with texture," she says. From antique cutting boards to organic, rustic modern plates, bowls, and vessels, her tableware props collection is exquisite.

I grouped these objects to show their creamy, milky deliciousness, to highlight the range of Pam's signature look and her tastes, and to fit her lifestyle. She is a wonderful cook, and the colors, textures, and aromas of food are poetry to her.

Quiet Alchemy

This room is a good example of the couple's style compromise. "Jim's dream is to have tons of art on the wall, salon style," says Pam, "while I like cleaner walls and visual breaks. I think because I'm a stylist and look at things all day, I prefer a quieter visual environment at home."

Both of them prize comfort, so they wanted to keep the furniture simple, easy to live with, and kid-friendly. Jim found the frame of the vintage chair in the left corner and had the cushions made for it using painter's canvas. The sofa is from DWR. The Eames rocker and the white cowhide rug mix sophistication and playfulness. "We live with the crazy kid stuff but sometimes hide it when we have company!" they say.

Unpacking Props

I snooped in one of Pam's prop bags from a recent shoot and discovered yonder organic baskets, bowls, and a cutting board. It screamed for display, so I created one to show how most of the time stylists have to work spontaneously with a color palette and within a textural context.

The Artist's Wife

A midcentury sideboard functions as Pam's vanity in the bedroom. As a finishing touch to an already beautiful arrangement, we piled up some ribbon rolls from her stylist collection for an even more feminine and undone sexiness. The black-and-white collage on the cutting board is by Jim. "I have a thing for simple graphics, subtly provocative imagery…and sexy vintage publications," he says.

Nature Morte

This still life expresses Pam's essential nature. In the creamy tones, the little touch of organic texture, the exquisite glaze of the small bowls, and the piece of baker's string, it's clear that her strength in decorating resides in the creation of amazing vignettes with personal objects and props. The watercolor pitcher drawing was a gift from Heather Chontos, the couple's friend and a fellow stylist. The bird drawing next to it is by Jim's younger son, Casey.

Simplicity Is Bliss

The master bedroom is still in progress....In the meantime, the couple do not mind its bare simplicity. The pair of chairs used as bedside tables were originally made for factory workers. Pam possesses a small collection of these so-called 'health chairs." She bought one from an interior designer friend and a second in a Miami antique store, and another friend found the third

one on the street in the West Village and gifted it to her. Too low and wiggly to be very comfortable, the chairs still delight Pam for their shape and their usefulness as the perfect side table. The old French café au lait bowls were a wedding gift to Pam and Jim and are part of a bigger collection. The bedding is all-white Belgian natural linen.

Creating a Focal Point

Jim's younger son from a previous marriage uses his bedroom only on weekends; it does double duty as Pam and Jim's office and props closet. The artwork on the wall creates the room's focal point. "Funkier, colorful stuff ends up in this room. These are a combination of my nineteen-year-old son Ryan's and my twelve-year-old son Casey's art. Some are just simple framed pages of their graffiti books. We clustered the more vibrant ones together to create a fun, visual overload type of look," Jim tells. His expertise in salon-style hanging is an art in itself and adds a playful wink of precision. The chest, ball lamp, and metal box all hail from Ikea, and Pam lent her sophisticated touch to the bedding set, which also comes from Ikea.

Texturing Tones of Gray, Cream, and White

Above a painted sideboard facing the dining table hang
various artworks by Jim. All of the sideboards in the room
were created from custom-made shelving units. They
were originally meant to be wall mounted, so Jim and
Pam had bases made for them. They offer a great way
to store Lily's toys and prevent clutter.

Talent definitely runs in this family! The guitar at
left was made by Jim's precociously talented son Ryan
when he was thirteen. On the other side, a cut-wood
trunk with its top painted in a creamy white lacquer
works as a stool or side table for books as art objects.

Stacking and Collecting

Danish modern, minimal, and earthy, the dining room corner is contiguous to the living room. The piles of magazines on the floor, which create a relaxed feeling, were inspired by a *World of Interiors* story. Art on the wall closely mimics the color tones and texture of the dining chairs. The table was designed by the late visionary graphic designer Tibor Kalman and one of his friends. Pam was his assistant at M&Co in the '90s and inherited the piece from his office. She has since managed to fit it into every single New York apartment she's lived in.

On the table, various antique glassware jars and some of Pam's favorite bowls hold pride of place.

Collages

The dining table also serves as Jim's worktable. The surrounding color palette seems so eerily coordinated with the color tones of the artworks that it is hard to decide which influenced which. Pam exclaims, "A perfect match! Especially now that the color palette of his art revolves around loads of beautiful tonal, neutral, and aged papers."

The highboy cabinet was a hand-me-down from Tori's parents' garage. The original finish was a high-gloss varnish. Tori sent it to be stripped, and the result is astonishing.

New Traditionalism
in a Glass Box

It's hard to believe this is Victoria's first apartment! Tori, as she is called, was a market editor at *Domino,* and we've worked on several interiors stories together. She has prodigy-like instincts, and her place is living

Victoria Jones

Chelsea, New York

proof. The rental that she shares with her brother in Manhattan is a white box in a nondescript luxury building. No architectural elements whatsoever, no individual character. The place's main asset is ceiling height—10-plus feet, which is fabulously rare for that kind of apartment.

By sticking with mostly traditional furniture silhouettes, piling on the rugs and textiles, and devising architectural sleights of hand, Tori turned a drab box into a sophisticated dwelling that would no doubt have impressed her decorating heroes, Albert Hadley and Frances Elkins— and her mother. "My personal taste has been majorly influenced by my mom, who collected such beautiful and unusual pieces over time—what I want to do eventually is get rid of all the placeholders and invest in timeless pieces that I will love forever," she says.

Tori once found a pair of cane chairs in a junk store. They were dull and green, but she reincarnated them by painting the frames light gray and adding fresh grass-colored velvet cushions left over from a shoot. Total reinvention! In pure Tori style, she gave a fresh twist to these traditional lines. She knows how to inject some bohemie into her twenty-first-century American classic interior.

Arabesques

Very often apartments have a "dead zone." Placing a tall mirror there is almost always the best way to go, especially in a small apartment, since mirrors expand the sense of space. The arabesque curves of this mirror add architecture that was lacking chez Tori. The X-base of the side table repeats that of the dining table. A little symmetry adds a lot of class.

Preppy Lacquer

Old books, creamy objects, black lacquer, and antique silver lend pedigree to any room. When I style vignettes, I group objects by a loose narrative—color palette, theme, etc.—and then throw in something totally unrelated to stave off predictability. Here, the purple wildflowers keep the still life from being too traditional.

Personalizing an Average Kitchen

In the fashion and decorating worlds, almost every designer approaches
a project by assembling an inspiration board. I find them to be unexpected
works of art—and in a home, probably the fastest, cheapest route to
personalizing a space (especially handy in a rental, when you don't want to
spend on permanent fixes). In Tori's mostly stainless-steel kitchen, her
board—a collage of postcards, magazine rip-outs, concert tickets, and other
keepsakes pushpinned to a corkboard—is a burst of boho esprit. Ditto the
ethnic basket, which does double duty as an extra pantry.

Reinventing Traditional Living

The rustic X-base dining table paired with reproduction mod chairs is a combination after my own heart. The collision of then and now creates intrigue that detracts from the bland corner. A rough-wood table provides historic heft while cheap-chic chairs (a plastic homage to the iconic Thonet chairs) tie in to the surroundings.

A bit of metal—the standing lamp and vintage silver candlesticks from a local flea market—deepens the material mix. We added little flights of fancy that have huge impact: the china set on the dining table and the windowsill assemblage of a mini topiary and a sleek shell. *J'adore!*

Architectural Symmetry

A genius touch to add to your styling file: Tori hung classical architectural renderings—inexpensive prints bought on AllPosters.com and custom framed—to give the illusion of architectural details. She instinctually knew to compensate for her apartment's lack.

Tori's furniture is mostly hand-me-down or big-box buys. She went for traditional shapes and colors to serve as placeholders until she can afford to upgrade. If you are still figuring out your style, this is the best way to go. (You still have to sit, after all!) The antique Italian glass lamps were her one splurge.

Coffee-Table Style

A few of Tori's favorite things beautifully displayed bestow instant chic. Stacking books and objects is another voilà-architecture trick, bringing sculptural depth to an area. Coffee tables can be one of the biggest decorating challenges. I prefer anything other than plain wood—stone, lacquer, mirror, glass. You can have a very average sofa if your coffee table is special. It's like wearing a pair of worn jeans and a white T-shirt with an amazing Marni necklace.

Sleeping Amid the Skyscrapers

The bedroom is floating among skyscrapers, which could be cold and disorienting. Overscale woodsy pieces, an old rug, and an upholstered bed are unexpected in a glass box, but they completely ground the room and give it gravitas. You don't have to live in a town house to emulate town house style!

Floral Romance

Tori was an art history major in college and collects art books. A loose bunch of flowers on a table covered with an old scarf and tomes feels fresh and unpretentious.

COLOR

When stylists get assignments, they are always given a color palette. It proves to be the underlying key to telling a particular story and establishing atmosphere. To me, every color has its own energy—blue is serene and expansive, red vital and warming, gray elegant and chic, yellow social and charming. For interiors, I find my way to color motifs through so many channels. Art, for example, connects me to color in a very primal way.

Robert Rauschenberg's "White Paintings" series (done with house paint, no less) helped me understand the endless possibility of white to impact a space, how it reflects light, how it gets cooler or golden depending on the weather.

Likewise, through Velázquez's portrait of Queen María Ana de Austria in the Prado I discovered the levels of depth of noir. I want to make a room out of the queen's dress! I have lusted after the violets of a Victorian boudoir and the crimsons of a Chinese palace glimpsed in movies I have long since forgotten, or the grayish blue-green patina of some Gustavian period furniture, and created whole decorating schemes in homage.

Color enhances, refreshes, and often completely reconfigures a home's DNA. Color can be used as a backdrop, as a punctuation mark, in an explosion, as a chorus, or as single notes. Monochromatic dwellings are as strong a color statement as a field of flowers. You can use a similar principle—using neutrals as a unifying thread—if your style choices tend toward genre hopping or if you inherited a mash-up of furniture.

If you like to take chances with color, draw inspiration from fashion magazines. I love how they daringly showcase "wrong" color combinations—a hot pink gown with a canary yellow clutch, or navy and black comingling in a Lanvin dress. Of course we all have favorite colors, or hues we feel totally allergic to. And color choices for interiors can be very tricky. You can love a French blue and be horrified once it's on your bedroom wall. You can loathe mustard yellow and be pleasantly surprised when you see it on a sofa. This happens to me often enough that I've deduced there are no rules for color. The key is really to make them work for your space—as the inventive homeowners in the following pages.

The bright white of this drawing of a folded napkin by Nan Kim reverberates amid the softer creamy kitchen palette. The vintage tray's dark edge becomes a strong linear graphic.

A Vision in White

I have always loved white on white, from Robert Rauschenberg's afore-mentioned "White Paintings" to the fashion designer Martin Margiela's all-white stores in Paris and New York. A totally white scenario reduces

everything to shapes and subtleties. I have this fantasy that one day I'll live in a *maison toute blanche.* I've thought of doing just one white room in my apartment, but I always chicken out. It's very challenging to create depth and geniality with this singular hue. Even with the best decorating taste it's easy to lapse into the clinical or overly ethereal. You have to decorate carefully to avoid a bleach-out.

When I visited Andy Gray's home, I was struck by how successfully he had achieved that hard-to-get warmth with white. Andy is the managing and creative director of design for an advertising agency. When he bought this nineteenth-century house in upstate New York, he assumed green would guide his interior—there was a lot of it already there. "In the bedroom, for instance, there were jadeite walls and maroonish floors, very grandmotherly and charming," he says. But during an endless renovation (four years), as he started to Sheetrock and skim coat the walls, everything turned a whiter shade of pale. Eureka!

A close look at Andy's house reveals many iterations of white, from plates to paint. In the Benjamin Moore Classic Colors deck, I count at least a dozen whites. Andy's canvas is Benjamin Moore flat white and a custom mix. "I bet I bought fifteen quarts. I wound up mixing the paint myself, and I finally found something I love, which is two parts Fine Paints of Europe (FPE) Antique Lace [cream], one part FPE Winter Sky [gray]," Andy explains. The creamier tone on the trim against the clean matte white walls conveys a new traditional sensibility. Select furniture pieces in black, bronze metal, and dark wood keep the house historically rooted and graphically engaging.

My aim chez Andy was to make the place feel a little more imperfect, a little more organic. Green reappears here and there, most notably with the sofa and chairs in the living room and in Andy's nature-themed art. I continued the outdoorsy ode by bringing in heaps of flowers from his garden. Of course, being blessed with such a resource for fresh blossoms, he can sustain this poetic visual trick long after the photo shoot.

Black and Noirish Green

The dining room is a wonder of simplicity and beauty. Andy bought the Thonet lab table on eBay for $20 and restored it for $300. The top is very faded brown Formica, so guests can drop food and wine on it without worrying. The black Paul McCobb dining chairs and the back door painted a noirish green break up the reign of ivory. The salon-style art display and the Arts and Crafts–style ceiling fixture are rustic counterpoints.

Seeing the Forest Through the Trees

This mélange of artwork has a common theme: trees. *Très poétique!* Andy has a graphic design background, and you can see how perfectly orchestrated the disorder is. The white frames link the grouping to the surroundings. All dark frames would have felt harsh. Throwing the plate into the mix is a break from the obvious.

A Chest of Drawers Has Its Moment

The baseboard-to-wall gradation of the paint in Andy's custom-mix color has a shadow-like effect, outlining the dining room. A restored wood chest adds an air of old-time sophistication. Although it's dark, its graceful silhouette keeps it from looking jarring. Andy normally just keeps a tray with the pair of candlesticks and his stereo on top of it. I switched the tray for the painting to introduce a little green to that corner.

'60s Chrome

Andy's vintage stove hails from a neighboring town. He bought it because he has a thing for the 1960s. (His loft in Manhattan is a paean to 1960s Danish modenism.) The chrome details repeated in the fan and teakettle function as a shiny, reflective riff on white, brightening the kitchen and ensuring that it doesn't veer into *Little House on the Prairie* territory.

Grandma's Jadeite and Brown

It looks like the green jadeite and maroonish-brown palette of the original grandmotherly bedroom found its way into the kitchen drawer. I like the unexpectedness of multihued silverware paired with white plates on a light table. I would add bistro-style napkins or unhemmed linen ones— in white, *bien sûr.*

Inspired Whites

The kitchen was formerly bright yellow, with a linoleum floor and a gray tile backsplash. Andy installed the wood paneling and painted it the same custom shade as the living room and dining room trim. Inspired by designer Ted Muehling's home, he doused the floor in a light gray paint that almost reads as white but avoids possible monotony. Andy stained the floors throughout the home is the same gray—an excellent example of color being the great unifier. I grabbed the distressed blue metal pail from the WC to celebrate the beachy tranquillity this kitchen conjures.

Acid Green Mixed with Stripes

T. H. Robsjohn-Gibbings chairs and the sofa (seemingly a Dunbar/Wormley copy) were both found on eBay. Their effervescent green fabrics recall the garden plantings and keep the palette fresh, while the metal cabinet and the stripped radiator have an industrial edge that makes the room less precious. Darker hues such as these and the brown stripes in the rug anchor the space— the white wall has no undertones, so light bounces all around. Hints of blue in the rug and the art provide some buoyant diversion. Andy stumbled upon the coffee table on Eighth Avenue when he first arrived in New York City. I love the capacity he has to see beauty in almost everything.

Greener on the Other Side

The former owner, who bought the house in 1929,
was an avid gardener. She tended a cornucopia of
unusual plants (heirloom poppies, rock garden peonies,
a big cactus, some beautiful roses, maidenhair ferns)
that Andy and his partner, Joe, chose to keep.

The First Taste

The garden surrounding the wraparound porch was planted with the help of several friends, notably Tony Bielaczyc, garden editor at *Martha Stewart Living* magazine. The green and white palette of the plantings is a prologue signaling what's to come in the home's interior.

Staging a Bright Intervention

Annie is the photographer for this book. She worked as a photographer at Christie's auction house, shooting everything from paintings to Muhammad Ali's boxing gloves. After assisting photographers, she struck

Annie Schlechter
Upper East Side, New York

out on her own to shoot interior and travel stories for magazines. If you ask me, she is also a closeted interior designer with a gift for color and a radical approach to it. Monochromatic schemes are not part of her design vocabulary. She and her boyfriend, Russell Maret, who runs a book letterpress, share a walk-up apartment on Manhattan's Upper East Side. With their architect friend Joe Serrins, they combined and remodeled two former rental units.

Brazen color rules the roost, with each room defined by its own theme. The living room features deep blue and dramatic pink that inspire lively chats; the bedroom is tranquilizing, with cooler hues plus hints of bright orange and soft blue; the dining area has a mellow elegance with taupe and pink décor; and finally, the kitchen-cum–cocktail area is a way-social yellow (yellow in fact appears in small doses throughout the apartment).

Annie's choices reveal how earthier tones balance the brights. Normally I think that neutral schemes are the best way to synergize varied furniture styles. But the high pitch of Annie's spectrum similarly acts as a common denominator, allowing her to indulge her love of everything from English traditional to Mondrian mod. I jumped in occasionally, adding little touches to underscore a tonal relationship or to undo a rare color discordance.

Homage to Yves Klein

Annie and her architect dismantled the warren of small rooms in the two apartment units to achieve a loft-like plan. The living room can be enclosed by two sliding doors contained within the blue wall. One big panel of color is less tyrannizing than a whole painted room. The wall is also statement art—the color references the French artist Yves Klein's famous Klein blue. Instead of clashing, the sofa ultimately matches the ferocity of the wall.

Saturated colors create cohesion out of eclectic furniture styles, from old-world (the sofa) to new-world (the coffee table and midcentury-modern chair, whose neutrality also helps create the balance). The rug is the perfect synthesis: an updated English classic floral pattern from the Rug Company in taupe and lilac.

For the finishing touches, I introduced a hint of green with the chinoiserie vase, playing off the wallpaper behind the bar. And I tossed a sheepskin throw from Ikea on the chair to prevent the color blocks from feeling garish. (The fuzzy texture and soft white mellows the blue, hot pink, and yellow.)

Stylist's Secrets:

Choosing Colors

* If your house has mostly vibrant tones from all the ends of the color spectrum, think of introducing small touches of neutrals to unify the look.

* To paint your house in neutral colors, mineral-based paints are best. With their subtler tonal shift, they change with the lighting for a very soothing and enlarging effect.

* Oil-based paint might be a pain, but it gives the sexiest finish: smooth, richer, and deeper.

* A panel of wallpaper used strategically can help infuse color into your interior.

* Framing a panel is also an excellent way to showcase swank wallpaper without incurring the expense of doing a whole wall or room.

The Match Jar

Annie felt the custom bookshelves didn't have enough presence, so she painted the stretch of wall behind them yellow. The books are not that colorful, but the solar hue performs a neat trick to enhance them. Sentimentality arises from the bucolic painting, the flowers, and the shells. Annie collects matches from all over the world and stows them in a jar. They deserved to be treated as a whimsical focal point. I also added the cube with the family photos to make the area feel more like a keepsake corner. That seems to be where Annie was trying to go.

Green Chinoiserie

The coffee table was reclaimed from the street, and Annie had a glass top cut to fit the dimensions. I like the scrap-pile-chic sensibility. There is nothing like stacks of books and flowers on a coffee table to make you feel at home. I shifted the pink and green books to the top, boosting the color scheme of the vase of peonies. Vintage dishes, fossil stones, and loose cards complete the unstudied warmth.

Horizonals and Verticals

I felt that the two vertical frames on the living room wall looked lost and random, since there is already so much verticality with the books and the standing lamp. The grouping needed horizontals. I'm an advocate of rupturing a pattern when it feels too repetitive. I wasn't crazy about the yellow and dark green combo, and ultimately neither was Annie, so I added the sheepskin on the armchair, which helps to cozy up the room. The lamp on the floor (the same lamp as the one in the dining area but with a yellow shade) is a wonderfully offbeat way to keep the eye moving.

Kitchen Couture

When Annie entertains, guests gravitate to the kitchen. (I know I do!) It has a gregarious design and a graphic color scheme that recalls a Mondrian painting, or a Courrèges dress. The blues and yellows link to the living-room palette, but the geometric application here is distinctly different. The refrigerator is hidden under the countertop, which serves as a buffet table during cocktail parties.

Baltic Seas

This little dining area, viewed from the living room, is a calming respite from the rest of the apartment. Annie designed the dining table herself. Placed atop a rococo side table, the lively mouth-blown-glass lamp disrupts the powdery pastels of this nook. Annie told me that this area is not finished, that she's not completely happy with it yet. Decorating is a continual evolution, and that's what keeps it interesting.

Black Frames and a Leather Pouf

This wall runs through the dining and living areas; its neutral color contributes to the airiness of the long open space. The off-white is also a good backdrop for Annie's salon-style art hanging. Sticking with black frames keeps the mix congruous, while the Italian tiles inject dimensionality. Annie plans to have the whole wall covered with art from floor to ceiling— the frames resting on the floor are waiting for a spot, but I love the unfinished, in-process note they add. I moved the Eames chair and the leather pouf nearby to strengthen the tonalities of the wall and the floor.

Striking a Red Note

In his office, Russell employed wine crates just stacked together as a
shelving unit and painted them white (hello, cheap chic!). Matching them
to the ceiling and the window trim makes them almost look like a built-in.
The combination of the white and the slate-gray walls is quite classical,
but the red desk and chair provide a rambunctious kick.

Bluebird

The bedroom is the most subdued room in the apartment. The cult "Woods" wallpaper from Cole & Son and the scroll motif of the bedspread conspire to create a fairy-tale forest effect. The taupe backdrop is calming but not lethargic, thanks to the optimistic splash of warm orange in the bedding and the low-hanging light fixture, which makes me think of a magical bluebird's nest.

Touches of Brightness

The bathroom is very graphic and simple, with a nod to old New York bathrooms. Russell designed the subway tile's motif himself. The primary-yellow bath mat and the equally vibrant green towel are low-commitment ways to go bright.

Sentimental Me

On the bedroom bookshelves, an unfussy grouping of framed photographs,
jewelry, and objects of sentimental value (such as the vase, which belonged
to Annie's grandmother) has nostalgic charm.

In this home, small doses of color punctuate
rich neutral surfaces and furniture.

The Neutral-Thread Formula

The New York City Chinatown loft that Nathalie Smith has lived in for ten years with her husband, John Zinto, is proof that a sweatshop can have a promising future. "We had to build out everything—walls, bathrooms,

Nathalie Smith

Chinatown, New York

and kitchen. All the windows had to be replaced and the red pine wood floor was sanded and pickled," says Natalie.

Nathalie and John kept industrial features like the tin ceilings and pipes, but their home reflects a penchant for warm, inviting modernism. A palette of soothing neutrals sets the stage for their collection of hand-made, midcentury, or vintage furniture and objects combined with rooms. Even though the raw space is made cozy with a spectrum of off-white, it never feels sleepy, thanks to energizing pops of strong color placed strategically throughout—most notably red.

A former fashion stylist for *Elle, Glamour,* and *Women's Wear Daily,* Nathalie now owns Global Table, a boutique in SoHo that is the tabletop mecca for every interior stylist in town. Many of her choicewares— modern vases, plates, and bowls in Easter egg colors—have made their way from her shop to her home. Nathalie's fashion past also instilled in her an uncanny sense of how textures sometimes define a color. She clearly understands how the underlying tones in neutral hues morph according to light, time of day, and the colors placed beside them. Because they play so well with light, neutrals have a very calming and somewhat enlarging quality.

It's a Family Affair

More minimalist than the rest of the loft, the kitchen was made possible by Nathalie's kin. The countertops are black schist courtesy of Nathalie's stonemason cousin at Ashfield Stone in western Massachusetts. Plates and serving pieces (mostly from her shop) line popular Ikea Lack shelving. "White walls look crisp with the more organic materials and show off the shapes of the bowls and plates on the shelf," Nathalie says.

Vintage artifacts—the taxidermied bird, the soup tureen on the shelf, almost bleached-out cutting boards—add personalization. The white, black, and silver/chrome palette creates a modern scheme while a few bright flairs are restricted to the shelf. Beauty is achieved through small but decisive touches, with an overall balance presiding.

Partially Hidden Treasures

As with Aladdin's lamp, goodies are contained in the china cabinet. When the door is opened, color bursts forth in this gorgeous mix of vintage and new china from Nathalie's collection.

Postindustrial Sleep

The walls of the bedroom are painted a pale gray from Benjamin Moore. By a trick of Mother Nature, the reflection of a nearby brick building bathes the room in an amazing petal-pink glow in the early-morning hours. The dark headboard is comprised of three panels of birch plywood that Nathalie and her husband assembled and ebonized. The small metal reading side lamps from Ikea are in keeping with the industrial-style loft. The couple made the bedside tables from thick planks of pine and metal stools. Artwork hung symmetrically in a variety of frames (mostly thrift-store finds) has a slightly Victorian bent. The cotton percale and linen bedding, bought from sample sales, shares the artworks' palettes. Leaning nonchalantly against the wall, a surfboard is a cool oddity. As the bedroom is quite small, functional chic was Nathalie's calling card.

Bedtime Stroll down Memory Lane

The tiny bedside table holds a trove of personal objects and postcards of Dorothea Lange, showing Nathalie's love of natural and worn textures. The rhino makes a stylish *vide-poche*. We added a bud vase—in robin's-egg blue—to continue the color-flash technique established throughout the loft.

Home Spa

In the bathroom, dark brown, light-colored wood, and hints of black and gray recall the kitchen palette. More Ikea Lack shelves hold beauty and toiletry essentials as well as bath linens. "I found towels (brown for my husband, white for me) that set the tone for the room," Nathalie says. Vintage touches such as the painting and the mirror bring charm to the cleanliness. The chic symmetry of the items makes the space feel quite luxurious.

Pale Fire

Nathalie felt the preexisting red brick was too '70s fern bar, so she painted it over in a chameleon creamy hue, Behr's Swiss Coffee from Home Depot. In the living room, the shade reads as bright white against a wall panel painted a Benjamin Moore crimson. "There was one Sheetrock wall in the living room, and it called out for color. Red looks good with everything (except green). It's warm and changes with the time of day," Nathalie explains. She employs the color throughout the loft to punctuate the sea of neutrality.

A theme of white, black, and silver confers casual modernity on the living room. Black-and-white gelatin prints, gifts from various photographer friends, relate nicely to the silver table lamps, the bowl, and the candlesticks on the bookshelf. The floor was originally red pine, which was dark and too rustic looking, so Nathalie had it sanded and pickled. "Light floors give the illusion of more space," she says.

A white slipcovered sofa against the red wall looks graphic and modern but still inviting. The armchair was originally covered in bright red cotton duck but has faded to hot pink—to Nathalie's great delight.

Modern Safari

Against the red wall, a detail of the Ikea Lack bookshelf displays a hand-carved wood rhino bookend. The orange vase is a Harry Dean glass piece from Nathalie's store.

Pop Goes the Bookshelf

Underneath a shelf of books and CDs, a neo-Warholian painting of mirrored
Empire State Buildings by Nathalie's brother-in-law, Matt Mullican, continues
the red wall's visual accent. The round raku vase on the wood chair is
another item from Nathalie's store.

A Beautiful Decorating Microcosm

Nathalie has a keen eye for details and instinctively knows how to compose with them. Except for the silver candlestick that she received from her family, all the objects here came from her shop. The composition is a small-scale representation of her decorating scheme. I added fresh irises and parrot tulips as animation, while the coral ring around the candle is a quintessential Nathalie touch.

The Silver Lining

The strong geometry of the black-and-white picture on the top alludes to the minimalist look of the kitchen. Displayed in a linear yet not stiff or crammed way, the objects relate to the surrounding nuances of the whites Nathalie has used.

With its minimal geometry and structural shape, the tower cube bookcase is a reference to Sang A's favorite artist, Donald Judd. The latex-covered sofa epitomizes sexy glamour.

An Apartment Fellini Would Love

The lady loves black (she wears it almost exclusively), but she lives in color. Sang A, whose namesake line of snakeskin handbags is highly coveted, and her husband, Jaime, a composer for film and advertising,

moved into their loft in Tribeca six years ago. They hired a contractor to redo the place and decorated it themselves. She says, "I liked the feel of the apartment with its eleven-plus-foot ceilings and the family-oriented neighborhood. I had a clear vision of what I wanted, and it was the perfect space for me to create my 1960s meets '80s aesthetic." At the time, Sang A was pregnant, so the place was designed to be kid-friendly as well as style-savvy.

When I first saw the apartment, I was struck by how it seems to explode with color, when in fact it is mostly outfitted in black and white. Against a mod black-and-white backdrop, pops of color in the form of key pieces of furniture and art float like bubbles, as if in a comic strip. Not that there isn't a serious design statement going on here. Traveling frequently to France and Italy, where Sang A oversees the fabrication of her bags, the couple cherry-picked all the furniture (they have pictures of themselves testing out the sofas and chairs in Italy!), including modern iconic pieces by the Campana brothers and Francesco Binfare.

Sang A had an illustrious former career in entertainment, as a TV news anchor, a miniseries actress, and a musician in her native Korea. It's not hard to imagine this apartment as the set for an avant-garde pop opera, with its rock-star bravura and fierce color choices: crimson red, bubble-gum pink, electric blue. No Old Masters color soul-searching here. Immediate and stimulating, that bold look telegraphs a "show" more than a "mood."

My main role was to tone down the overly dramatic moments. The task was to unify and simplify in order to keep the apartment from reading cartoonish, while maintaining its audacity. The furniture placement was also a bit random. I moved around a few pieces and edited others out, to give what remained more breathing space and power. In a big room with scant furniture, the placement of those pieces is key.

Who Are You, Polly Maggoo?

Talk about dramatic entrances. Walking into the überglam, graphic hallway, one feels like an actor in a performance. Sang A says her décor was inspired by Fellini's *La Strada* and by William Klein's faux-vérité spoof of the fashion industry, *Who Are You, Polly Maggoo?* The mod, recessed lighting is cinematic, too. Behind the doors with the frosted Plexiglas circles is a closet for coats and shoes—a mudroom in hiding. The black-and-white geometric references swing from the '60s (the floor) to the '80s (the door). Sometimes such geometrics can be dizzying, so I like how the veins in the marble floors balance them with an organic vibe.

Butterflies and Campbell's Soup

The kitchen is the nexus of the apartment, where the family spends endless hours together, eating, talking, working, watching television, even falling asleep (Olivia!). Karim Rashid butterfly chairs and a vintage checkered Formica table recall a '60s diner nook. Touches of color—the turquoise on one chair and the hits of red in the background—provide ample energy without overwhelming. Olivia's rainbow drawing tacked to the side of the cabinet, the board of family photos, and the hanging Campbell's-soup-can light fixtures are the sort of lighthearted infusions that I just adore.

Grand Dining, Twenty-First-Century Style

The freestanding Plexi "wall" separating Jaime's office area from the dining zone bursts against the graphic backdrop. Its curved shape and transparency, paired with the ultramodern take on crystal chandeliers (Swarovski crystal clusters) and the banquet-like dining table conjures the drama of Sang A's beloved Fellini film.

Robin's-Egg Blue on the Sill

A little styling makes a moment. Before, these exquisite blue Ted Muehling vases looked lost and lonely. I introduced one white ceramic vase with a perfect round shape, as big as the sum of the three others, to serve as an anchor and balance out the sweetness of the blue, and suddenly this still life has purpose.

Techie, Traditional, and Mod Converging

Adding the robin's-egg-blue tufted chair in this living room corner grounded the vases on the windowsill. This corner needed some love! It was my personal homage to Antonioni's *Blow-Up*—in which English traditional and mod converge—but Sang A was happy to oblige. I like how the audio system is just hanging out. Sometimes we surrender to function over form, and in this hyper-designed room the stereo strikes an appealing practical-guy note. (Sang A let her husband have his toy!)

No Strings Attached

The living room has a strong point of view. "When I design, my palette is always black, so my floors had to be black. This allows my art and furniture pieces to stand out the way I like to see them," Sang A says. Essentially, she is accessorizing with color; just as a fuchsia clutch accents a black dress, the bold accessories are what grab attention.

The anemone chairs by the Campana brothers are not that big, but their statement is overscale. I placed them more centrally, as the room needed this kind of presence to fill the space. As I styled, I moved furniture and objects so they would appear to float as in an art installation (thus putting the furniture under the proverbial spotlight).

Kissing the Bride

A snapshot of Sang A and her husband, Jaime, on their wedding day sounds a sentimental note amid the polished décor.

The Melody Maker

An unintentional connection between Jaime's music studio and the living room suggests itself. The black leather desk chair and the Kiss album here remind me of the '80s rock moments there (the black leather sofa and the lips painting), and the audio wires even link to the string chairs. Part of being a stylist is to observe peoples' instincts and help articulate them.

Fashion Lingo

When we shot the apartment I became obsessed with Sang A's closet.
It is like a museum of the best pieces of the last few decades. Amazing
Balenciaga dresses and shoes, Stella, Chloé, Prada, all packed in a happy
mess. Sang A may be unaware of it, but her clothing sensibilities carry
over to her living room—these strong pop-arty flashes in a black sea.

IVAN TURGENEV
FIRST LOVE

OB-JECTS

Objects are the secret language of a home. They transmit intimate messages about the inhabitant. The presence of an object, ugly or pretty, is justified by the owner's connection to it. They can have sentimental value and relate to memories, or they can be chosen based on sheer beauty, humor, purpose, uselessness, or simply mysterious appeal. In the stylist's world, *l'objet* is king. We like to construct stories with objects, create a world around them, manipulate them to define a space or complete a lacking corner.

On the other hand, too many things can verge on *Grey Gardens* madness. They need to be curated, edited, and displayed wisely.

We group items of different size and shape according to a color thread, a nature theme, or poetic randomness, or we place a spare object in prime position all by itself. The guiding principle may or may not be overtly perceptible, but it nonetheless telegraphs import and meaning.

Homes feel generic without these bits of soul. In styling a home that is bland, I will usually bring a few objects and build the décor with and around them. Integrating something intense and strong or even borderline gaudy can completely turn a room around, creating a nice tension and bringing a focal point to the room. On the other hand, if your home has a lot of remarkable objects, editing them can give each more weight and bring cohesion to the room.

Sometimes objects respond to one another naturally. The best pairs are often ones that are slightly different but complementary. The owner's eye can sometimes find a common thread in a bunch of found objects with no relation in style or color. That's the case with my Italian friends in this chapter, whose house is an homage to the souvenirs of their wanderlust and intrepid flea-marketing. On the other hand, a boutique-owning couple from Brooklyn, New York, hews to a gothic scheme for their extensive, exclusively black-and-white collection of objects. In an upstate New York cottage, well-worn artifacts play off midcentury modern architecture. Last but not least, my dear Parisian friend has a more art-gallery approach, appointing her apartment with spare furnishings and vibrant pieces that are given ample room to stand out. It is amazing to see how these distinctly different approaches all yield strongly defined interiors.

A surrealist exhibition of biker's artifacts displayed in the entry sets the stage from the moment one walks through the front door.

Black, White, and Goth All Over

Eva and Gentry's one-bedroom garden apartment in Brooklyn adheres rigorously to a simple noir scheme, from the furniture and books to their closets and the clothes within. No colors cross the threshold, save for the

Eva & Gentry Dayton
Brooklyn, New York

occasional bunch of pink peonies. The couple is abstemious when it comes to furniture, too. The interior revolves around the couple's very peculiar collection of objects: Gentry's ever-growing stash of

skulls, crosses, old religious books, and biker's helmets, and Eva's stash of buddhas, jewelry, and delicate clothing.

While macabre in theme, the apartment exudes an elegant calm. That's partly due to the schematic polarity of the objects themselves—masculine/feminine, black/white, hard/soft, redemption/damnation—and partly because of the symmetrical, precise displays. Balancing one another without canceling out one another's strength, they create a sense of calmness and simplicity.

I'm fascinated by the thoroughness of Eva and Gentry's aesthetic, and by their ability to define their home through these singular oddities rather than through the color of the walls, which are white, or through the furnishings, which are black or dyed black to create a uniform look and make them recede. Of course, when you put objects front and center, styling is essential. Eva and Gentry have an incredible sense of the relationship between objects and spatiality. I didn't pitch in here at all—I was scared to move anything! I felt that the slightest shift might bring the minutial, intriguing order tumbling down. Their approach is opposite of mine, which is more instinctual. The more I agonize and contemplate, the more lifeless the result. Not so with Eva and Gentry. They invest thought, time, and energy and produce exquisite artistry.

Eva says their main décor inspiration is fashion designer Ann Demeulemeester's store in Antwerp, a temple to austerity. Fashion is a huge influence on the couple—not surprisingly, as it happens to be their day job. The husband-and-wife team owns the cultish namesake shop Eva & Gentry, a cutting-edge fashion boutique near their home in Brooklyn. They designed the space themselves, and Gentry just finished designing the new Helmut Lang store in New York City. For Eva, who graduated from the Art Institute of Philadelphia, "art feeds fashion, and fashion feeds art." Without question, fashion clearly feeds their interiors, too.

Simplicity Rules

Eva and Gentry took advantage of a closet to carve out a small home office. Symmetry is dominant: two chairs, dark skulls framing the white one, old army blankets dyed black and used as cushions on two vintage metal school chairs. An array of brass candlesticks of varying heights breaks the dual pattern. This is simplicity at its best—not boring, but edgy. The symbol of purity of the calla lilies on the floor and the delicacy of the pink peonies on the desk bring to mind the death of young Ophelia and the dark romanticism of Edgar Allan Poe.

Mercurial Thoughts

Eva has had this midcentury-modern chest forever and feels that she has
outgrown it. "If only I could replicate it in steel. It's the perfect size," she
says. I agree it is out of synch with the scheme of their home. A painting by
Mitchell Hoffmaster is more in tune, with an eerie beauty that is further
enhanced by the nearby stark lamp.

Rock Artisans' Wardrobe

His and hers: Eva's inner Hollywood circa 1930s femme fatale balances out Gentry's Darth Vader chic throughout the apartment. For Eva, clothes are like sculpture. Her favorite designers are Rick Owens and Ann Demeulemeester, both known for strong, sculptural clothes that wrap and layer around the body. But she has an attraction to girlish feminine accoutrements as well.

An Eastern Bent

On Eva's side of the bed, objects are grouped around symbolism and texture. The buddhas and om sign were bought in India. The block print (bought in Paris and used for carpets), the agate stones, the elephant tusk, and the bead necklace share an organic quality. The lamp adds a high note. Eva and Gentry don't like purely decorative objects. "Objects need to have meaning," she says.

A Dark Mannerism

On Gentry's simple metal bedside cube is a glorious goth shrine. He has been collecting skulls and crosses for the past five years. Eva says, "When Gentry gets into something, he gets into it full force." The intensity is toned down by the elegance of the display. A handblown glass skull anchors the assemblage, while the repetition of the small brass skulls and various crosses creates order and unity. Dainty chain necklaces and a rosary draped around the church candelabra confer the sensibility of still life by Il Bronzino (had he painted still lifes!). This sixteenth-century Italian painter's brilliant mannerism came to mind when I first saw the nightstand display because of his haunting way of rendering beauty and reality.

Marching to That Noir Drum

In the living room, black-dyed army blankets appear, here covering music equipment on the floor. The owners intend to keep this decorating touch. Everything from the midcentury leather sofa to the animal hides, like the lamb skin at left, marches to the noir drum, but the airy white curtain brings calm. The round wood-block coffee table amplifies the lodgey, convivial note of the animal hides. It stands its own ground like a Brancusi sculpture. Of course, the couple wants to replace it because they think it's too organic. They envision something in steel and glass.

Heavy Metal

Gentry bought an old bike engine to custom build a personalized ride. The unfinished machine in the living room looks like a heavy-metal homage to Marcel Duchamp. On the Mies van der Rohe Barcelona stool, neatly folded military blankets, with their connotations of war, further the barbaric elegance and the goth scheme.

Near the entrance, a coatrack crafted by Mauro displays a hat with a string cord from the Dolomite region in Italy, a hat from a flea market, and hammocks from the Yucatán. Rusticity links the items.

Arte Povera Bliss

Four years ago, Michela and her husband, Mauro, bought a small nothing-special house upstate. They had no desire to undertake lengthy renovations, but wanted simply to make the place suitable for weekends in the country as quickly as possible.

Michela Martello &
Mauro Bareti
Upstate New York

There was nonetheless a major soul infusion—with very little money shelled out. The couple has traveled extensively, and their décor is essentially a collection of souvenirs, alongside family hand-me-downs and their own handicrafts. Call it wanderlust décor. The house contains items dragged back from the foothills of the Himalayas, the African continent, even the streets of New York. It has a laid-back warmth and a safety that only worn and cherished objects can confer.

This place could be somewhere in the pampas of Argentina, or somewhere in Umbria. It has a part hacienda, part Italian-country style. Michela and Mauro barely even repainted, just refreshed the living room with white paint. They even kept the old-fashioned wallpaper in the guest room and bathroom, appointing the house mostly with found furniture and objects brought back from trips or picked up at flea markets. "We like antiques and objects we collect around the world. I love paradox, things that don't have any relationship but that next to one another create a kind of harmony," Michela says.

They added a big deck in back, where they enjoy Campari drinks on warm summer evenings, and turned the original porch into Michela's painting studio. Michela started out as an illustrator for children's books and now creates murals and mixed-media paintings. Mauro is a former fashion photographer who now owns an Italian restaurant in the West Village.

When she first came to New York, Michela and I met through mutual friends we have in Italy. Straightaway I liked her free spirit and Italian sense of humor. She and Mauro, also an Italian expat, have such joie de vivre. They have exported their Italian lifestyle to New York — they zip around on Piaggio scooters, love good food, and are the most hospitable people.

Michela's grandfather was an antiques dealer, so perhaps that explains her attraction to objects with a former life. The couple are not afraid to enlist anything to create ambiance — leather boots, Michela's paintings, hand-stitched dolls.

Common Denominator

With the worn leather gear on the ladder and the leather boots beneath, a whiff of an Argentine hacienda sneaks through the entryway. The painted cabinet was found on the street in front of Mauro's restaurant in New York City. I moved this painting by Michela from the living room — I couldn't resist putting those feet here by the boots. The Indian style of the painting ties in to the white Indian shawl and the punches of color in the books.

Blue-Wall Infinity

Michela and Mauro loved this original blue paint in the bedroom so much they left it as is. The wall-to-wall coatrack was handmade by Mauro, based on a primitive version they saw in an antiques store. On it they hang bags, clothes, and sundries (there are hardly any closets in the house, so they had to pare down to prevent the place from being a mess). The bedspread is from Botswana, and Michela hand-painted the bed frame with Buddhist iconography and images. Despite the vast, global range of styles, the elements are unified by their geometry, earthy colors, craftsmanship, and of course the enveloping blue paint.

Stylist's Secrets:

Editing and Curating a Collection of Objects
Choosing one theme or one color can help tighten the look even if they all hail from different aesthetics and periods.

* Unleash your fantasy and throw a couple two-cent black flea market vases to your black basalt Wedgwood collection. It will uplift the group and give it unique charm.

* To avoid the crazy bazaar look, display only the objects brought back from travel that you love, and use them sparsely.

Assembling a Soulful Room with Found Objects

An inviting, den-like unpretentiousness pervades the spacious living room. Everything speaks to chilling out. On the walls, two of Michela's paintings emphasize the back-to-nature theme. The couple found the black Eames chair on a New York City sidewalk—what a score! The African drums are for play and decoration. Michela and Mauro are very comfortable with the randomness of their eclectic taste. When a home revolves around objects (as opposed to architectural elements and decorative flourishes), the layers of décor can feel more organically evolved. The result is an intuitive, emotional comfort.

Alliteration

Pattern repeats in the old quilted throw on the sofa, the urn on the floor, and even, loosely, in the Tibetan carpet.

Medicine Cabinet Extraordinaire

Michela painted the watercolor of the sunglasses and tennis ball for Mauro, who is a tennis player and aficionado. The fashiony chic of the art contrasts with the old-fashioned floral wallpaper (original to the house) and adds some funk to the bathroom. A piece of handmade lace from a small island off of Venice has been transformed into a toilet-paper holder!

Puppet Master

The little Argentine doll strung from the shower, a gift from a friend, nicely plays off the colors in the wallpaper. This is an example of how everything finds a place in the Baretis' home, creating a small imaginary theater.

Portraiture

Michela sews on paintings in her studio, where a Heriz carpet and a Victorian footstool on the green floor ensure a cozy vibe.

Tools of the Trade

This is a perfect image of how ordinary tools of the trade become decorative objects conveying the most soulful poetry. The mixing palette was hanging on the wall of Michela's studio. Just moving the wood paintbrush holder, which was sitting in the other corner of the room, next to it creates a tableau, and the pair starts to tell a story. Most of us have beautiful, meaningful, or interesting objects scattered all around the house. Bringing them together by theme, color, or shape in a strategic part of the room (for example in a forlorn empty area or in a corner that needs a little zing) creates a stronger moment and enhances their beauty.

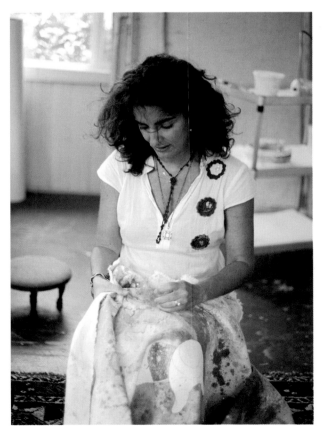

This drawing is a remembrance of
Phil's childhood summers at the
Woodhall Oceanographic Institute.

Lamellibranchiata. Unio.

A Midcentury Cottage with Storytelling Soul

At the end of a dirt road, half hidden in the woods, a midcentury-modern house of glass and stone peers out at a nearby lake. Inside, the upstate New York home of writer Cynthia Kling and her journalist husband, Phil,

is filled not with sleek furniture but with artifacts from all over the world.

After living for more than ten years in an old stone house, the couple took a leap and moved to this modernist dwelling designed by Minoru Yamasaki, the World Trade Center architect. While Cynthia and Phil love midcentury architecture for its beauty and functionality, they find furniture from this era to be quite uncomfortable and didn't want the house to look like a mini temple to midcentury design. The furniture from the previous house was a mix of weathered pieces, along with art and other treasures scooped up on various travels, primarily in India and Africa.

Cynthia majored in anthropology, so objects have a very special meaning and place in their home, which has few actual walls. The living room and kitchen are part of a large open plan, and most of the surrounding walls are glass. The challenge was to make their belongings feel natural in this contemporary environment. What caught my attention when Cynthia enrolled me for some house styling is how the keepsakes and furniture dictated the color palette throughout their home, not the other way around. That chromatic unity is what ultimately solved the paradox of the antique objects versus the modern architecture.

Inner Calm

The kitchen stove with the dog drawing and antique clock above conjure country-life charm, while the big glass windows bring nature into the interior. Clean lines in the kitchen allow Cynthia's antiques to breathe so the room doesn't become cramped quarters. The window seat is an ideal spot for reading and delighting at the outside lushness.

Old Look, Brand-New Kitchen

Cynthia and Phil bought the house as a shell and retrofitted the kitchen from scratch, including built-in cabinets with a countryish feel. The green and yellow mixing bowls warm up the space. They adapt via their color palette, which plays up the hues of nature in full view.

To Keep or Not to Keep?

A few steps down from the kitchen, the large, open living room looks out onto a small deck and the woods. The honey tone of the floor gives the room an even sunnier outlook. Near crammed bookshelves, a nineteenth-century *recamier* (a lounging bench that originated in France under Napoléon's reign) creates an informal library area. Left on the floor, the lamp next to it exudes a bohemian feeling. On the other side of the living room, piled-on ethnic rugs and cushions accent the sofa and 1950s armchairs. The light and open space is filled with warm, well-loved, comfortable furniture. On the window ledge, a piece from Cynthia's collection of Hudson River paintings leans casually against the glass.

"Happy to Be in the Same Gang"

As beautiful and natural as the palette of this home is, having too much of a similar thing can make a room feel a little *triste,* or melancholy. Bright touches of color help chase away that feeling.

In a corner of the kitchen stands a cabinet bought in Pondicherry, India. The yellow pot on top is a piece of traditional pottery from Provence, France. The yellow vase was bought at Barneys New York, and the painting at an antiques store in the region. The mementos hail from such different places, yet match perfectly. I placed a simple flower arrangement by Cynthia in the mix.

Stone, Wood, and the Indian Maharaja

The stone wall has such a strong presence that we put this portrait of an Indian maharaja above. Its delicate rendering, the mineral colors, and the gold frame confer a painterly quality on the stone itself. The rawness and minimalist simplicity of the wood steps leading to the kitchen repeat the stratums of the stone, while the two smaller artworks mirror the ascent of the staircase. The metal sign is an apt description of the place.

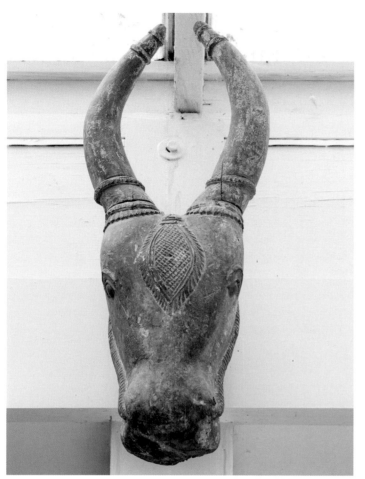

Sacred Cow

A cow head from India rests under a skylight in the kitchen and looks like the benevolent deity of the hearth. The antique wood imparts an ageless texture to that corner. In this home, it's easy to travel (mentally…) from the bank of the Hudson River to the ghats of the Ganges River.

About Charles Darwin

On her desk, Cynthia employs keepsakes for practical purposes: a small antique African wood pot and a Darwinesque piece of pottery crafted in Vermont are now pen (and feather) holders. The African vessel was brought home from a trip to Botswana Cynthia took with the scientist Kathy Payne.

A Hudson River Palette

Cynthia mixed three custom colors for the house using Benjamin Moore paints. The key was to mix these three colors together, making them slightly darker or lighter when needed. "I chose colors connected to my perception of the Hudson River," Cynthia says. In the distance, the bedroom shows its bright side. The bedding, rug, and chest extend life into the long narrow hallway.

The New Neutrals

The poster bed was custom-made for the couple by a carpenter in Connecticut. Sunny quilts and pillows plus the bright green lamp keep the warmth all year round. "For me, neutral colors include yellow, orange, green…and browns and blue…and red!" Cynthia enthuses. "Neutrals are the ones that relate the most to nature." The early-American blue trunk at the foot of their bed holds linens. The bedroom makes you feel like you're sleeping in a tree house.

Mossy Haven

In the bathroom, moss-green tiles on the wall and the beautiful wood-slab bench that Phil made tie in with the outdoors. Patterned ethnic bath linens feel homey and add a sense of hammam exoticism. An old-fashioned bathtub, a gift from a friend (former *Domino* magazine editor in chief Deborah Needleman) is situated to provide a perfect view of the woods. While everything here is worn, organic, and vintage, the sparseness of the room has a Zen quality, and that funky gold radio tunes into twenty-first-century cool.

Warming the Stone

The old woodstove in the bedroom is original to the house. We leaned the gold-framed print and hung one of Cynthia's collection of Hudson River paintings to offset the magnificent rawness of the slate. "I love the stone visually. It reminds us of the antiquity of life," Cynthia says. We also used a primitive American wood bench as a bookshelf to add some gravitas.

Charm School

A wonderful host, Cynthia created a welcoming guest bedroom. An oil painting (also Hudson River School) is united in poetic simplicity with a yellow vase filled with spare stems of Queen Anne's lace. The vase is set upon a nineteenth-century mirror atop an antique-marble–topped chest. "Little vases allow for the examination of the flowers," says Cynthia.

Various trays from all corners of the world complete the kitchen décor. I love Véro's idea of recycling an old paint palette as a tray—another way of looking at an object.

A Poetic Stance in Paris

Véronique is what you might call an object-o-phile. She cites the Swiss duo Fischli & Weiss among her favorite artists. One of their best-known works, the film *The Way Things Go,* features an explosion of flying objects crashing around. Véro's devotion to this aesthetic plays out at home.

When she settled with her family into this Paris apartment ten years ago, she avoided decorating it. She is more dedicated to travel and decadent dinner parties than to décor. This is a family that lives in the moment. The girls have grown up, but the apartment still has a transient look and an adolescent attitude. I encouraged Véro to pull it together a bit! Most everything was unearthed from her closets, cabinets, and boxes. Véro's place became the perfect lesson in how to create décor on the fly. That is often exactly what stylists have to do.

"What I find moving in an artwork is the accident, that slightly off feeling and the questions it brings. That's why I like mixing things up, like an old piece of furniture loaded with history and a contemporary object that doesn't have a past yet," Véro says. She has no definitive style beyond a love of vintage and bright eccentricities.

Véro is also a bit of a decoration-phobe. She grew up in a château on the bank of the Saône river, near Lyon. She used to be terrified at night when she would see the toile de Jouy drapes moving in open windows. Now she hates drapes!

Her apartment is a three-bedroom in classic Haussmannian style (high ceilings, moldings, French doors, parquet floors, and at least one fireplace) located not far from the Canal Saint-Martin, an artsy neighborhood in the heart of Paris. Véro has worked as a photo editor at *Jalouse* and *Beaux Arts* magazines and has a passion for images.

In spite of the scarceness of decorative objects in Véro's home, each of them offers a strong narrative and a natural presence through the way I chose to juxtapose them.

Je Ne Sais Quoi

Véro's apartment has such regal architectural details that a Spartan décor confers more importance on the little things. The fireplace, with its ornate molding in the Louis XIV style, is the pièce de résistance. Interestingly, Véro doesn't want art on her walls. "For a living room, I like white, near-empty spaces, which give life to the objects and spark reflection about them," she says. Sometimes it's nice to put all the objects away and go back to them, as Véro does, to refresh the eye and the interior.

On the other hand, her living room called for some cohesion. Véro had one of these '50s chrome and plastic chairs, and our friend Marie-Laure, a set designer, hooked us up with the rest of the set at the Clignancourt flea market. The dining table hails from Véro's family home in Lyon and folds up into a small desk.

I wanted to get rid of the side table in the corner to tighten up the décor. Its scale seemed wrong and it looked a bit lonely. But Véro fought me valiantly. The side table was her grandmother's. When you love something, you can (almost!) always give it a raison d'etre.

The flower-branch light on the wall from Habitat is a gift from her younger daughter, Siam.

Indian Bunny

Like a cheap and playful riff on a Jeff Koons sculpture, the inflatable bunny (bought from a stylist who carted it back from India) resembles a piece of modern art. Small things actually have huge impact chez Véro, because of their individuality and brazenness.

Market Place

In contrast to the relatively subdued living room, the tiny kitchen bursts with color. Véro's parents gave her the brandy glasses and decanter. The glass bottle with a soccer player in it was brought back from her partner's grandparents' house. The little bag with the Madonna is from Mexico and goes with the happy green. Each time I visit the kitchen, the mood-enhancing quality of these knickknacks strikes me.

Some Fresh Red Roses

The French windows open onto a balcony *fleuri* (plentiful potted plants and flowers)—quintessentially Parisian. The roses on the dining table were found at the local *épicerie*. Sometimes a simple bunch of flowers is enough to completely lift the corner of a room.

A Flowering Theme

In the living room, the wood coffer holds fabric and a tablecloth bought in India. A flower light from Habitat designed by model/photographer Helena Christensen gives an air of pastoral poetry. We plunked flowers picked up at a nearby *marché* into a zinc vase we found buried in the kitchen cabinets. I love the simplicity of a tall vase with flowers in a spare room. I repeated the flower scheme (the balcony, the light fixture on the wall, the fireplace carving, and the flower light on the coffer) to create an idea of abundance without heaviness.

Magic in Little Things

"What I like about them is the story they tell," Véro says about the old offering boxes given to young brides.

Improvising Glam Rock

Choosing a sofa can be the hardest decision! I hear that concern again and again. I often use fabric as a quick fix. Véro's cat destroyed her living room sofa, and she is still trying to choose what to replace it with. She showed me a shiny silver swatch that she had stored in a trunk, so off I went to the Marché Saint-Pierre in Montmartre to buy more of the fabric. We could have gone with an elegant piece of natural linen, but this honors Véro's sense of humor—and the disco glam of the '80s (it also has a Warhol Factory vibe). The glass lamp with the chartreuse silk shade further sparks the electricity.

Spilling It Out Loud

This vignette is the result of a mini archeological dig through Véro's apartment.
I propped up the magazine cover for its graphic power and transported two
votive holders from the dining table (that appear as if they are spilling out
of the mouth!). Véro's grandmother's hand-painted vase softens the tableau.
The vases further the 1980s glam of the sofa fabric.

MOOD

Ambiance, atmosphere, aura—an interior without these is like a cake without icing. We French are definitely moody! Mood is a physical and emotional sensation as much as a visual one. It is cinema-tographic, alchemic, diffused, hard to pin down, poetically charged. Upon entering a home you may be struck by a feeling of peace, coziness, spaciousness, or even movement. A moody home has a strong narrative and layers that reflect the multifaceted personality of the resident.

We've all had the experience of entering someone's home and being shocked by a mood and personality disconnect. A lot of clients ask me to align who they are with where they live.

Mood doesn't just emanate from the way furniture is arranged, or color choices, or a decorating scheme, though those can all be part of telling a story. It's also in the objects, books, travel souvenirs, plants, textiles, art—anything with a sentimental connection, history, or meaning—that function as Proustian madeleines in a home. It's the sum of everything.

Think of the spaces that trigger your emotions or stimulate you profoundly—that surreal feeling during a night stroll in Venice, the memory of soothing blue-gray in a summer cottage, or a glimpse of vertiginous red on the wall of an Indian palace. That's what you want to go for at home. That je ne sais quoi that gives a space its unique soul, making it the ultimate place to rest and recharge.

How do you achieve this sense of soul in a home? Not just by lighting some scented candles, painting your bedroom sky blue, or buying all midcentury-modern furniture. Some of my styling tips are to create layers through textiles and fabrics, to avoid an overly homogeneous theme, to showcase your cherished objects and art, and to keep collecting new things. But most of all it's about confidence! Trust what you like, and don't worry if other people don't approve. Let your inspirations guide you, since those are usually indicators of the narrative that resonates most for you.

In the following homes, you'll see four interiors with very distinct moods: a modern wintry fairy tale, a Jean-Luc Godard–worthy lair, a Scandinavian haven, and an English cottage retreat—all in the heart of New York City! These apartments will show how to script narratives around a central theme, with a dose of fantasy, *bien sûr*!

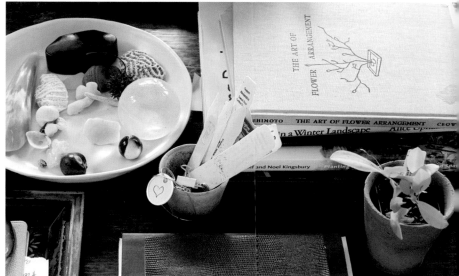
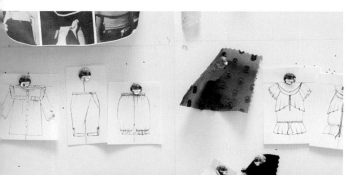

The carefully selected objects in Tom's apartment share a white, cream, and gray palette. The painting makes the other objects seem more earthy and less precious.

The Ice Storm

Tom has an amazing eye for interiors, honed during his long stint at Sotheby's researching and selling in the furniture, tapestries, and contemporary art departments. More recently decorating editor, he is now

a bona fide interior designer. His West Village apartment is in a three-story brownstone. Even before you notice the beautiful décor, you are struck by a feeling of serenity. The apartment has a fairy-tale quality, all icy and blue and light—like in a Hans Christian Andersen story. The tranquil ambiance is achieved through a harmony of cool neutral tones and a spare orchestration of furniture and objects, grounded by Tom's exquisite taste.

Tom says, "The décor was dictated by the house's bones, which are Italianate." The neoclassical narrative plays out in dialogue between choice antiques, classic modern designs, and cool art—all in a Nordic palette. The grand architecture includes high ceilings and spacious rooms, which Tom intentionally chose not to fill completely. His restraint creates an eeriness that is more tranquilizing than frosty. "I grew up in *The Ice Storm* New England," Tom says, referencing the Ang Lee film. "In a contemporary house in Connecticut in the 1960s and '70s—all glass and wood." Yet he has a cozy side, too. "My family had a groovy A-frame in Vermont, so I have a soft spot for anything that resembles a ski house," he confesses. To be honest, there wasn't much for me to do chez Tom. More to learn, really!

Icy and Blue and Dreamy

To balance the Victorian bones, Tom intervened with modern tables and an oversize paper lantern. The repetition of the Saarinen tables, one higher, one lower, creates a lovely flow between the living and dining areas.

Tom filched the George Smith sofa from a friend who was getting rid of it: "He was sick of hearing me hem and haw about what sofa to buy." The chairs in the foreground were bought at Sotheby's for $800. "They were purple and dirty but catalogued as Billy Baldwin. I had them reupholstered and found out they're signed, so now I'm very smug about them," Tom says.

Tom would have preferred to lose the drapes, which are left over from a photo shoot, but the beautiful old windows do next to nothing to keep out cold and noise. "The drapes are too girly, but I can't get it together to replace them," he admits. I put the helmet on the chair to remind us that we are in the twenty-first century. I could sit on the floor drinking tea for hours in this room. It has a meditative quality, like the hush of freshly fallen snow.

Ice Storm Revisited

The small Milo Baughman side table was bought on eBay. Chrome, glass, and white cowhide equal ice-storm glamour.

A Very Chic Cave

In the bedroom, a cozy, nonlinear cluster of framed works is unobtrusive yet poignant. There is also an intimacy in the art choices, hanging quietly in a corner above Tom's dresser. The Italianate molding could make the room feel too grand, but Tom chose dark gray (Benjamin Moore's Chelsea Gray) for the walls to foster a more intimate scale. "I think we are meant to sleep in caves," Tom says. "I know it sounds bratty, but my bedroom is too large, and I felt lost in the space when it was white."

Italianate Touch

The sconce and the fireplace (and that gorgeous molding) are original to the house. The minimalism of the bedroom prevents the fixtures from looking overly meringue-ish.

Reductive Romanticism

Demonstrating Tom's respect for patina, a pair of eighteenth-century
Louis XVI chairs bear faded fabric, while the radiator is left raw to make
the place feel less precious. "I always want to strip things back to
their essence, without stripping away the life and soul. What would you
call that…reductive romanticism?" Tom says with a laugh.

The Heights Dictate the Lines

Built-in bookshelves house Tom's extensive collection of art tomes. Scaling almost up to the ceiling, the shelves' neoclassical lines extend the height of the space. Keeping the books fairly loose in their arrangement prevents a stiff library feeling.

Babe Paley's Kitchen Chic

The galley kitchen is a great example of how to give a soulless spot flair.
The light-gray walls are outfitted with minimalist Ikea Lack shelves
showcasing a well-edited collection of kitchenware, ceramics, and the
occasional art piece. "I am highly sentimental about objects, and the art
I have is things that moved me for some reason, because they are beautiful,
thought-provoking, or funny. A home needs those things," Tom says.
I totally agree! The *bouillotte* lamp (an eighteenth-century French style with
adjustable candle brackets) once belonged to Babe Paley—very inscuciant
of Tom to stick it on the kitchen counter.

Cherry Blossom Bliss

In this tiny galley kitchen, the crystal cherry blossoms of the Tord Boontje
chandelier contribute to the fairy-tale story line. Tom had a long obsession
with this fixture. "I made a pilgrimage to see it and dreamed about having
it. I finally found it at a Christie's Interiors sale!" It majorly dresses up
the kitchen. Pink and gray is a combination made in heaven. So poetic.

Office Corner

Tom's home office is part of his bedroom. Situated by the glorious windows, the computer faces an elm tree outside. A clean white palette for a workspace keeps the mind clear, and the sage plant lends some life. Even Tom's screen saver has an Old Master vibe.

Ethereal White

Tom painted his floors white to hide the unfortunate orangey pine that was there. The light playing off the floors casts an ethereal glow.

The synergy between rustic and science
fiction seen here could be a Paul Ritter
signature.

The Multicultural Loft Odyssey

When French fashion designer Alice Ritter first moved to New York, she lived in a small, dark studio. On a brief sojourn in Paris, she met her husband, an English-American design director who had been living in the

Alice & Paul Ritter
Brooklyn, New York

City of Light for twelve years. They landed in a 1,000-square-foot loft in Williamsburg, Brooklyn. Eight years later, they are still enamored with it.

Alice and Paul stuck to the fairly simple bones of the rental apartment. They had the walls painted white and made no major structural renovations or additions except for the kitchen.

At first glance, Alice and Paul's decorating tastes seem to be at two different poles—masculine and feminine. His: insane collections of Japanese toy robots, vinyl records, guitars. Hers: delicate porcelain and objects. "I come from a French bourgeois background with a love of distressed and unusual objects. Paul is more modern. We are always striving for a minimalist look, when our natural characters tend to accumulation!" Alice says. Alone, her choices might read as a little too sweet and girly, and his could have evolved into overgrown-boy madness.

Instead, they've turned their home's interior into the perfect equation of modern, whimsical, and welcoming. "Growing up, we had two living rooms; one was barely utilized—only when guests were invited. I really don't like the idea of a room being so formal; it's very important to me that my apartment be useful and comfortable, a place to relax," says Alice.

Breaking the Grid

Wall-to-wall windows in the Ritters' loft bring in beautiful light and make the space seem larger. All-white walls and unfinished honey-colored wood floors provide a neutral backdrop. The sofa with an Italian design bent is from Design Within Reach. Bookshelves running the length of the wall give the room a soulful layer. A chandelier that Alice bought at a flea market confers a girly touch that balances out the more industrial elements of the loft.

"I love midcentury minimalism, but if that's all there is, I find it stifling. It needs either a rustic or a romantic note, an eighteenth-century chair, something to break the grid," Paul says, in tune with his wife's touches of whimsy.

Stylist's Secrets:

Giving a Space Soul
Effortlessly beautiful homes always happen organically. Let the space dictate the décor, then force some of your obsessions on it to give it soul.

* As objects of decoration, books are always a winner in conferring coziness on a space.

* Tightly organize volumes on bookshelves for a tailored look.

* Loosely pile books on floors or a coffee table for an artsy bent.

* Don't be afraid to to against the grain. Mixing and matching styles with confidence will give your space a unique mood.

French Frou-Frou and Far Eastern Pop

A golden amphora vase flanked by a portrait of Marie Antoinette and some Japanese cartoon character figurines provide a glimpse at the sense of humor that reigns in this household. "Contradiction is the essence of human nature, isn't it?" Alice declares with typical French sass.

The Porcelain Menagerie

Little porcelain animal figurines with a pastiche charm are displayed on an Eileen Gray glass and chrome side table from Design Within Reach. This grouping perfectly sums up Alice and Paul's taste range and their love of contrasts. The monkey is from Lladro and was purchased at a local cultish store, The Future Perfect.

Art House

Found at a local antiques store, the metal coffee table serves as the stage
for a rotating display of Alice and Paul's favorite art books of the month. They
are passionate about art, books, music, and film. One of their most beloved
activities is to go to galleries on weekends; what they see translates into their
space. I styled this scene to show the owners' color sensibility: "dusty pinks,
creams, colors distressed and faded by time."

A New Kind of Shabby Chic

This whole black moment is a loose homage to being French and living in Brooklyn. A tongue-in-cheek Starck faux–Louis XVI Ghost chair nestles up to a painted trunk bought in a junk store around the corner. Halfway rustic chic, halfway Depression-era poor, the scene is jazzed up with a gold Harry Allen piggy bank and a hatbox with a ribbon and bow. Of the trunk, Alice reveals, "I don't know where it originally comes from, but I have imagined a story for it ... it used to be part of the trousseau of a young bride, probably a peasant girl, and it traveled with her in the countryside."

Dividing Space

Alice and Paul separated the office side of the loft from the living and kitchen area with bookshelves full of magazines and a glass cabinet holding an action-figure collection. This creates a small passageway to the bathroom, a clever solution for keeping some areas more private. In another artsy touch, Paul posed on the floor a framed poster for a Michael Thompson photography book he designed a few years ago.

Feminine by Contrast

Both Alice's and Paul's desks are situated at the entry of the loft, next to a walk-in dressing room and beneath their loft bed. Alice's is a natural extension of her work. "My fashion line is feminine, classic with a twist, casual and comfortable, as should be my apartment."

This area draws its sunny disposition from the skylights above. The metallic touch from the entry door is carried through in the desk, lamp, and chair.

Alice warmed up the white, boxy corner with delicate drawings, various black wood frames, French folk costume paintings, and her own fashion sketches on the wall.

Flowers and Stars

On the other side of Alice's desk, a photograph of the couple in Paris sits next to a set of woodcut stars bought on eBay.

Superfriends, "Star Wars," and Loud Guitars

A music fanatic, Paul once worked as creative director for Virgin Records, France. His passion is apparent in his office, where he displays his all-time-favorite album collection.

Because the toys, figurines, records, and other goodies are all neatly contained on shelves, they read as great decorative accessories rather than clutter. The highly graphic and theatrical mix is not unlike the universe created by one of Paul's favorite artists: "Stanley Kubrick had a huge influence on my visual tastes in terms of interiors (and design in general). My taste is pretty much based on the final scene in *2001: A Space Odyssey*, when Dave Bowman arrives in the ultra slick modern room with the European furniture."

Virtual World

Directly opposite the hallway bookshelves, Princess Leia and various toy robots mingle with beautiful old framed prints and nineteenth-century black wood boxes. A recurring powdery blue tone unifies the objects.

I WANT YOU TO JOIN THE POSSE!
!GIANT!

PATÉ DE
CAMPAGNE

French Propaganda

Next to the kitchen counter, a white faux-antique, wish-it-was-real chair from Oly Design strikes a romantic French bourgeois note. The *"pâté de campagne"* butcher sign, tree branches with birds on them, and the hint of a baroque silver candelabra extend the theme, and the little touches of bright red in the bowl and the propaganda poster keep it modern and fresh. A fortunate result: the kitchen cabinets, which were in the apartment before Paul and Alice moved in, are elevated by white paint and the inspired design and now seem in keeping with the provincial French style of that corner.

Midcentury Dining

Just opposite the kitchen sits a midcentury Danish Hans Wegner dining set bought a few years ago at a neighborhood antiques store. Organic warm wood and rope seats in the chairs counterbalance the slicker parts of the loft. The baroque silver candelabra adds femininity and hints at the effortlessly chic dinners Alice and Paul hold.

While Lindsey's apartment is just 500 square feet, the terrace adds another 350. In the summer, the garden becomes her living room.

An English Garden in a Tiny Penthouse

Have I stumbled into a cottage off the coast of Wales? Lindsey's studio apartment may be in Gramercy Park, but her charming aerie has a fireplace; cozy, rustic décor; and a wraparound terrace bursting with old-fashioned roses, peonies, and lavender.

A garden designer, floral stylist, and inventor of modern terrariums, Lindsey grew up on a farm in Canada, and she brings her pastoral past to her now distinctly urban life, giving it a quintessentially British twist. "Merchant Ivory films, Miss Marple," she says, detailing her inspirations. "And my travels, my family, my friends, *The World of Interiors.*" She naturally gravitates to the lovingly aged. Yet there is a clean, modern infrastructure—when she bought the place eight years ago, she redid the floors in oak, installed modular white cabinets, and painted the walls in regal neutrals. Nothing dank and dusty here!

Lindsey is also a natural stylist. She creates exquisite vignettes out of found objects, nature's bounty, art, and artifacts. As a result, her home feels as if everything is charged with memory, bottled and translated into décor. Her terrace ultimately defines the place: "I don't know if I'd still be living in New York if I didn't have that terrace. I'm too claustrophobic. When it rains, you actually hear the rain land. When there's wind, you hear the leaves rustling. That's a real luxury on the eleventh floor!" she says. She spends winters by the fireplace, and the rest of the time basically lives out on the terrace. The line between inside and outside is practically nonexistent.

The Foyer Is the Kitchen

The teensy kitchen is situated in the entryway and quickly sets the tone for the apartment. Despite its size, it is very well organized. The zinc sink and metal cabinets have a slightly 1950s look. In lieu of drawers, Lindsey stashes her silverware in pots lining the counter and windowsill—very informal and country.

The simply framed bird drawing by Lindsey's young nephew is one of the few color notes in this placid home.

Pretty Bowl Obsession

A detail of the shelves showcases the earthy texture of the porcelain bowls (in front) by Francis Palmer. They are made with a very unusual glaze. "I use them for everything. I love the texture and the glazes. They are like little paintings you can hold in your hand. I'm crazy about bowls. I can't get enough of them. Maybe because they usually get filled with something comforting," Lindsey says.

Goodness!

Linens stored on open shelves add another layer of homespun goodness.

Tea at Lindsey's

Spices, tea (indulging her inner Anglophile, Lindsey buys lots of Harney & Sons), and bottles of oil and vinegar are neatly arranged on shelves, which serve as a miniature pantry.

Urban Cottage Style

The kitchen window offers a view onto the terrace, where Lindsey set up a trellis covered with ivy and planters filled with herbs. The petite dangling heart, the old-school coffeemaker, and the ironstone bowl complete the picture-perfect frame.

Cabinet of Curiosities

Lindsey found her "cabinet of curiosities" at the vintage design shop and decorators' mecca Beall and Bell in Greenport, Long Island. "I like a home with a great mix of art—contemporary, old, personal odds and ends. I look at a painting and think how I could turn it into a garden or a flower arrangement, using the mood, colors, textures," Lindsey says.

The black-and-white collage by her friend James Gallagher adds quirkiness. The central oil painting here, with its black background, anchors the eclectic mix and creates a visual magnet (the eye would otherwise go in every direction because there is so much going on inside and outside the cabinet) and links up with the repeating black to create unity. Black always introduces sophistication to any interior. The bright yellow stool is the counterbalance to the heavier earthy tones.

Still Life with a Blue Vase

Lindsey's natural styling instincts are apparent here. She created this gorgeous still life around the Italian renaissance portrait of a young man, which is fraying at the seams. It sits half hidden behind a vase with a similar blue as its background. The different textures of the vessels, the zinc container with the smudged sage, and the translucent crystal ball make a richly layered tableau. *J'adore* the lupine flower stem set effortlessly in the little porcelain bowl.

An English Garden on the Inside

Imported from the family farm in Canada, the cherrywood dining table faces the terrace and moonlights as a desk. An assortment of old chairs, two vintage lamps, and the baskets scattered along the edges of the floor keep Lindsey in a bucolic state of mind. An antique chest that once belonged to her grandmother acts as a file cabinet. The wood spear in the corner is part of a primitive African bow and arrow.

Lindsey's furniture is cleverly arranged so that the room doesn't look crowded: The dining table takes up as little space as possible but doesn't look tucked into a corner as it is parallel to the floor-to-ceiling windows. On summer nights, Lindsey carries the table onto the terrace for alfresco dinner parties. Her apartment looks just like the gardens she adores: It has informality in formality.

Weathered and Well-Loved

On the dining table, even the tools of Lindsay's trade are chosen for their beauty and displayed with panache. The twine, garden books, and notebooks look like they have been here forever. Her work-related items are mixed with shells and glass paperweights that share a weathered and well-loved quality. Everything has its place—the tray, the bowl, and the plank serve as elegant frames to host her things. The sprout is waiting for a sunny spot on the terrace. You have entered the world of a gardener!

The Feng Shui of a Cozy Living Room

Lindsey's beloved sofa faces the fireplace, and together with the rug, a gift from friends, delineates the living zone from the dining zone. The rug's stripes also make this area feel bigger. The high stacks of books have a cocooning effect from the vantage point of the low-slung sofa. The city is also successfully kept away, and Lindsey makes sure that whatever she misses about country life is replicated in spirit here—from the log pile to the big feathers and wood bark in the glass jar on the shelf. Next to the jar is a light created by her boyfriend with a bunch of neon tubes.

Nature Ephemera

On the fireplace, a nostalgic vignette comprised of scraps of nature mixed with sepia photographs transports you to that seaside cottage. The flower frog turned feather holder is ingenious. A tiny black skull strikes a punk note in this memento mori narrative.

Zoë looks like a young Anna Karina in Godard's *Pierrot le fou*. "I find these flowers both sexual and silly — the lovechild of Georgia O'Keeffe and Dr. Seuss," she says.

Cinema Verité in an Alcove Studio

I asked Zoë to write this book with me since I have always admired her writing style, wit, and flair. We met when she was the features director at *Domino.* As I was selecting houses to include in the book, I wanted to

Zoë Wolff
Chelsea, New York

show a few that are defined above all by the inhabitant rather than by the décor itself. Zoë's is a prime example. Expressing personality is a big component of a stylist's job. It's like decorating for your soul. Stylists tease out or create moments that in turn give places their particular mood.

The first time I walked into Zoë's apartment I was struck by its laid-back feel—a little rock-and-roll, super cinematic, and not-so-secretly romantic, too, in a British (her heritage) and French (her obsession) kind of way. It's easy to imagine the heroine of a Jean-Luc Godard movie living here. In nouvelle vague films, the characters always seem to live in apartments or houses that have a transitional quality but at the same time, are unquestionably dynamic on their own. An accumulation of details— a piece of art, the color of a certain lamp, a stack of old books—speaks to the character and in turn projects a poignant mood.

Like the owner's whims and desires, everything seems to be in constant motion chez Zoë, as if her apartment contains scenes from a film. The haute-hodgepodge décor isn't predicated on awesome furniture but on individuality and constant questing. *Très existentialiste!*

Zoë is a Libra and admits she is typical of her astrological sign: She loves beauty and has a very difficult time making decisions. She sought guidance from me in buying new furniture and synthesizing the styles in her apartment, which is in a landmark building in Chelsea. It's an alcove studio blessed with elegant molding and all-day-long light streaming in from three windows running along one wall.

Zoë gave me inspirational tear sheets from magazines, and we discussed her likes (and dislikes) over a breakfast of tea, croissants, and fresh raspberries laid out on her coffee table. We came up with a loose decorating plan—not an easy task, since Zoë's sensibility is restlessly diverse, influenced by everything from a Gerhard Richter palette to Jane Mayle's old Nolita shop (RIP) to a classic sexpot image of Serge Gainsbourg and Jane Birkin. One day she wanted a traditional English sofa, the next she questioned whether to go more modern. She wasn't sure about whether to wallpaper her bedroom, paint it a darker color, or leave it alone. She was proud of the modular Vitsœ shelving unit she had splurged on but apologized for her behemoth TV. We made some strides with a new sofa and dhurrie, but welcome to her eternal work in progress!

Napoléon III and That Denim-Blue Rug, All in the Mix…

Zoë's friends' artwork, like this painting by Erica Nicotra, plays a dominant role in her 450-square-foot studio. "I love to create a community at home with pieces that remind me of a person or place," she says. The tones throughout the apartment are similarly warm, with a lot of dark wood vintage pieces, ethnic textiles, and oatmeal hues (in a small apartment, too much tonal variation can create claustrophobia). The Napoléon III sofa was re-covered with natural linen. The sky-blue dhurrie speaks to the boho traveler in Zoë. The armchair is 1940s French and a gift from your humble author.

Romantic Sleeping Nook

The bedroom is nestled in a little nook. Zoë wanted a headboard, but we opted for a piece of art as an approximation. I knew it needed to be a photograph, ideally contemporary, something not too sweet, so it could keep the bedroom on edge. The movement in the photograph by Zoë's friend Coke Wisdom O'Neal is in line with the cinematic ambiance of the apartment. Her bedding is simple and fresh: a bit organic with the textured white duvet and satiny blue throw, a bit English with the floral pillow. She's had that fleamarket side table since college!

Undone Cool

A family drawing set on the floor has a lovely informality. The portrait of the lady—her South African grandmother—reflects Zoë's roots. One of my favorite styling tips: Art sitting on the floor and leaning against the wall conveys a nonchalant romance. The Sinatra CD cover in the background has an old LA vibe.

Saying It in French

If Zoë's place had a sound track, it would probably be a song by Françoise Hardy (that's an old 45 on her bookshelf), Serge Gainsbourg, or The Kills.

A Personal Touch

The kitschy horse, picked up at a vintage shop in Palm Springs, California, serves as a bookend. It adds a sense of dynamic movement to the shelves. Under it, the picture of Zoë and her dad looks like a still from a Wim Wenders movie.

A Cinematic Kitchen

This kitchen really speaks to me! Iconic magazine tear sheets, concert stubs, art postcards, and a photo of Zoë's mom pregnant with her (center) grace the fridge. The small rug, bought on a trip to Marrakech, channels Zoë's inner child of the '60s. The hand towel has a homey touch and continues the pink theme. Dark walls—Benjamin Moore's Ocean Floor—create depth. Zoë decided on this rich color because the kitchen was such a nothing space, with sad cabinets and counters. Well done, mademoiselle! Now it oozes old-world charm. This room is the ideal blend of everything Zoë is.

Bent Metal Note

A wrought-iron chair from an amazing vintage furniture store on the North Fork of Long Island adds an ornamental, gardeny note in keeping with the natural light of this apartment.

By Way of London Calling

The bathroom is very atmospheric. If you didn't know where you were,
you might think London. The powdery purple wall and the black trim and
checkered-tile floor share a romantic patina. The windowsill of the
bathroom serves as a vanity and fits the home's script. "I'm really into smell,
and just looking at these bottles conjures memories," Zoë says. The art
on the wall by Zoë's friend Willy Somma evokes *mystère.* Who is this girl?
Who lives here?

DASH OF STYLE
(The last touches)

A few small, smart touches might be all a home needs to add the final panache. A pottery lamp on a wooden table can do wonders. So can a bookshelf sprinkled with unusual and beautiful objects, such as a bird's nest and a sculptural Maarten Baas vase. Coffee tables, side tables, or dinner tables become magnified with accessories like a brightly colored runner or something as simple as a big bouquet of black tulips in a white porcelain container.

In a series of eye-candy shots, I'll show you how different styling permutations and some little tricks can turn a house around by bending or just loosening up those old conventional decorating rules a bit.

SIDE TABLES

It's all about the lamps

Lamps help set the tone for a room's décor. Choose side lamps carefully, using them not only as practical tools but also as beautiful objects. Keep in mind the finishes of the lamp and the surface it will be resting on when you decide where to place it.

Opposite. An everyday desk lamp takes on new life in the living room. I wanted to pair something a little unexpected with the traditional sofa and neoclassical drawing.

Above. This lamp is highlighted by the metal table but would get lost on a bone-colored one.

Left. This white ribbon lamp was purchased at the Habitat store in Paris. Here, volumes are at play and geometry was the keyword. The square side table, the wood block, and the small painting in the back suggest how a past geometry class translated unconsciously into my dwelling. Inspiration comes from every part of our psyche.

Sometimes it's just about the tray

The secret to keeping your stuff neat and organized on a coffee or side table, trays can be used as a frame around any collection.

Below. Trays work best when they have a small lip to prevent the contents from spilling out, enabling drinks or nuts to be placed worry-free on the table.

Unexpected options

Think alternatives: Flea markets and junk shops are full of great old boxes and other objects that can be transformed into stylish side tables. Your old metal trunk found in Paris could be a wonderful and surprising solution for that lost, uninspired corner of your living room.

Above. And what about that wooden oddity you inherited from your grandpa's fishing cabin? Turning it into an occasional table will add warmth and a cool Adirondack touch to a room.

In the world of styling, anything goes as long as you can thread it all loosely together to keep it cohesive.

SHELVES

The many lives of bookshelves

For practical reasons, some people like to line bookshelves with books only, neatly organized in rows and arranged as in an office or a bookstore. If your inclination leans toward a more personalized look, bookshelves can also be an excuse to display family photos as well as original or sentimental objects.

Below. Create a slightly bohemian Parisian look by mixing objects in with the books on your shelves.

Right. Think about creating an assemblage on your shelves, pairing iconic and neo-classic objects as bookends. Note that the objects and books mix styles and eras. Keeping the case open enough will allow each piece to breathe.

Above. If you are looking for a more classic and beautiful but still subdued look, keep all the objects on the shelves in one color scheme. For instance, group everything in different shade of blacks or grays, or in varieties of whites, or whatever else piques your fancy. Arranging your books by color, as Lauren Goodman did in her apartment (see pages 54–55), can stimulate your interior with mini visual fireworks.

In the kitchen...

If you aren't naturally neat, kitchen shelves that are open can easily turn into an unsavory sight or a big bore. Try adding some fantasy with colors and poetic objects. It is possible to keep open shelves organized and functional yet give them a whimsical touch by putting together tins, cans, and containers with their own graphic integrity.

Opposite. Use large, pretty porcelain or metal jars to store dry goods. A trick to keeping the containers organized is to stack them in large colorful cubes, like the red and blue ones in the background (they can be found at kid's stores).

Below. If your plates are on open shelving and, like mine, are mostly of the same color family, break up the visual with a few brights. My French café au lait bowls add the perfect zing to these shelves. Maybe your old-fashioned teapot or the set of colorful mugs brought back from your trip to Lapland could serve the same purpose.

The accidental shelves

Living in a home with very little closet space? The accidental shelf can be a great option for storing, displaying, and styling.

When I needed an extra shelf, I found it very handy and decorative to use the top of a hutch or cabinet. To keep it from looking hodge-podge, I chose all clear glass vessels that repeated the glass of the hutch doors.

TABLE-
TOPS

Table settings

Sometimes a simple runner can make all the difference. Even when setting a table for dinner with friends and family, I like to let my imagination run off the beaten path and use whatever is available to create a theme.

Below. You can make your own tablecloth with chintz left over from your drapes, old French linen bought at a European flea market, or even a piece of raw silk from Bangkok.

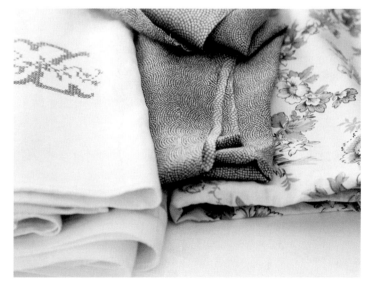

Above. For a more (but not too!) quiet and formal setting, vintage ornate silverware and crisp linens will bring good old continental flair and an Emily Post feeling to the table. You can add a pair of crystal candlesticks to take things up a notch.

Opposite. To make casual bohemian feel sophisticated, I'll mix luxe linens with bistrolike plates and flatware and place loosely strewn flowers and greenery around the table.

An easy bar setup, effortless and sophisticated

I like to set up bars on trays so they can be moved around to various locations, depending on the event. When I am hosting my book club, I set up the side table in my office as a bar. A few bottles of wine, glasses, and a couple of candlesticks usually do the trick.

FLOWERS

A room is truly alive when it contains living things (in addition to you, of course). No matter how exceptional the furnishings, photos, artwork, and objects, there is nothing like trees, flowers, and foliage to increase the pulse of a space. A simple bunch of flowers can be the decorating flourish without which a room feels unfinished. Flowers can add extra color to a kitchen counter, lend dimension to a collection of objects on a bookshelf, or uplift a drab corner.

My friends and clients often express being intimidated by flowers, especially when it comes to artfully incorporating them into a design scheme. Don't worry about crafting a flawless bouquet or finding the perfect table centerpiece—work with what moves you. From a miniature terrarium housed in a basic fishbowl to a one-bloom bouquet, the lightest and most unexpected touch can make all the difference. My French compatriots will probably jail me for saying this, as flower arranging is like haute couture in my home country, but similar to decoration in the House of Diallo, bouquets know no rules! Let yourself be carried away by what delights you and follow your bliss.

Here are some tips to get you started.

* Statement bouquets and branches. All-white calla lilies or tulips in a tall glass or off-white ceramic cylinder work wonders on a console or even on the floor. Branches tend to be voluminous so keeping their vessel minimalist will enhance their lines. They confer a simple elegance, which elevates more mundane rooms or corners. Grand branches add drama and flair when you host a party and can be placed on a pedestal column for the full effect.

* Bedroom whispers. On the bedside table, a loose bunch of fresh-cut wildflowers in a Chinoiserie vase will bring Bloomsbury style to your nights. You can put this together in two seconds, keeping it lo-fi and light—the stylist's way.

continued...

* Recycled chic. For small arrangements, I like to use whatever petite vessels can hold water as little bud vases. I prefer the unexpected—a former jam jar, a colored vintage drinking glass, some cool minimalist pottery from a hipster store in Silver Lake, Los Angeles. On my desk in my home office, a small antique blue glass bottle bought at a local junk store for nothing with a single white garden rose peeking out gives me instant happiness.

* Dinner-party philosophy. A dinner party lends itself to low bouquets in small vases so that people can carry on a civilized conversation without having to peer at the other guests through a wild bush of greenery. In winter, flowers like chartreuse or dark purple hellebores in a bunch of little vessels can be scattered the whole length of the table, creating an organic runner. Intersperse tiny clear votive candles for a crystalline touch. In the spring or summer, line the table with ivy or branches and set up two (to five) tall silver candelabras if your table is big or one in the middle if it is small. Voilà, Shakespearean decadence!

* A touch of Babe Paley prep. Inexpensive blue and white porcelain flowerpots that you can find at your local Chinese emporium make wonderful vases for big bouquets in the summer. Place a plastic container inside to hold the water, plop in some fresh-cut white sweet pea blossoms, and you'll import that East Coast preppy look directly onto your kitchen counter.

* Over the top. For a festive cocktail party, I'm into an orgy of multicolored flowers in big gypsy arrangements—like what you see in the hyperbolic photographs of Tim Walker—set on a wide and long console in the middle of the room with the bar accoutrements. Too much in this case is never an issue. The ephemeral nature of flowers makes them even more spectacular, and we should enjoy them as much as we can.

* Buying the flowers. I typically decide what to use when I'm at the market the morning of the shoot, depending on what is fresh and available, and bien sûr, on my mood. I gravitate toward certain flowers. Don't ask me why, but I love hydrangeas, cherry blossom branches, old-fashioned roses, and peonies. And I'm not afraid of carnations if they are all that is available at the local deli. As a photo stylist, I've learned to work with many circumstances. I adore wildflowers and completely fall under the spell of hellebores' evanescent beauty. My favorite colors are white, pale pink, and (sometimes) hot pink. These colors adapt to almost every interior.

* Smart blooms in the salon. Midsize arrangements with bold flowers such as peonies are beautiful on a library table or coffee table, or on top of a pile of books. Bulbous-shaped vases with an open neck look best for this kind of bouquet. A cream ironstone pitcher looks just right filled with hot-pink peonies. Or try a round crystal or Wedgwood pitcher for an effortless aristocratic look à la Duchess of Devonshire.

* Picking the vessel. When styling shoots, stylists have a very short amount of time to compose arrangements. Whether the goal is a single flower in a bud vase or a big grouping of branches, the first thing I decide on when looking at the scouting shots of the house are the vessels and their height, style, and color. It's important to make sure the vases will complement or enhance the place or, if the space is already overly decorated, disappear (or blend) a little into the background. Vases will tie the flowers you choose to the interior.

* Down to the ground. A tall vase with magnificent flowers such as dark (papillio) amaryllis resting on the floor becomes an exotic botanical object. I place them near a fireplace, in a dull corner of the living room, or even on the bathroom floor next to the tub. In the bathroom, I also love orchids for their slightly poisonous beauty. Very sexy, indeed.

Acknowledgments

To my beloved family, and to N.N. and his family.

Huge thanks to all my friends whose homes are featured in this book: Rosemary Hallgarten, Victoria Jones, Lindsey Taylor, Pam Morris and James Gallagher, Eva and Gentry Dayton, Michela Martello and Mauro Bareti, Nathalie Smith, Cynthia Kling, Sang A, Lauren Goodman, Andy Gray, Annie Schlechter, Véronique Rautenberg and her family, Alice and Paul Ritter, Zoë Wolff, and Tom Delavan. I am grateful for all I learned from them.

And again, very, very special thanks to dear Zoë Wolff, badass writer, for teaching me how to write, and for her masterful and brilliant editing. Unbound gratitude.

My deepest appreciation goes to the former editors of *Domino* magazine, Deborah Needleman, Sara Ruffin Costello, and Dara Caponigro, for their mentorship and for sharing with me their knowledge, and to decorating guru Tom Delavan for his inspiration and kindness.

Very special thanks to my editor at Clarkson Potter, Aliza Fogelson, for her guidance, help, and unwavering support. I feel that without her this book wouldn't have been possible, and I can't thank her enough. Very big thanks to my agent, Carla Glasser, at the Betsy Nolan Agency, for her constant encouragement and for making this happen. Thanks to the amazing Jada Vogt, for her major help and assistance in photographing the Zoë Wolff, Pam Morris, and Alice and Paul Ritter stories. A big thank-you to Cynthia Kling for her help editing the last chapter. A very big thank-you to Lesley Unruh for her generosity and contribution on the "Dash of Style" photography.

Where to Find It

Furniture

ABC HOME
888 and 881 Broadway
New York, NY 10003
(212) 473-3000
www.abchome.com

AERO
419 Broome Street
New York, NY 10013
(212) 966-1500
www.aerostudios.com

ANTONY TODD
260 West 36th Street
New York, NY 10018
(212) 367-7363
www.antonytodd.com

ARMANI CASA
www.armanicasa.com

BDDW
5 Crosby Street
New York, NY 10013
(212) 625-1230
www.bddw.com

BEALL AND BELL
430 Main Street
Greenport, NY 11944
(631) 477-8239
www.beallandbell.com

BLACKMAN CRUZ
836 North Highland Avenue
Los Angeles, CA 90038
(323) 466-8600
www.blackmancruz.com

CALYPSO HOME
407 Broome Street
New York, NY 10013
(212) 925-6200
www.calypso-celle.com

CHAPMAN & RADCLIFF HOME
517 N. La Cienega Boulevard
Los Angeles, CA 90048
www.chapmanradcliffhome.com

CONRAN
www.conran.com

FLAIR
88 Grand Street
New York, NY 10013
(212) 274-1750
www.flairhomecollection.com

GEORGE SMITH
315 Hudson Street
New York, NY 10013
(212) 226-4747
www.georgesmith.com

HABITAT
www.habitat.co.uk

LANEVENTURE
www.laneventure.com

OCHRE
462 Broome Street
New York, NY 10013
(212) 414-4332
www.ochre.net

WEST ELM
www.westelm.com

Textiles, Rugs, and Wallpaper

B&J FABRICS
525 Seventh Avenue, 2nd Floor
New York, NY 10018
(212) 354-8150
www.bandjfabrics.com

BENJAMIN MOORE PAINTS
www.benjaminmoore.com

CAROLINA IRVING TEXTILES
80 Church Street
Englewood, NJ 07631
(646) 688-3365
www.carolinairvingtextiles.com

CAVERN HOME
195 Chrystie Street
New York, NY 10002
(718) 766-5464
www.cavernhome.com

COLE & SON
Lee Jofa, Inc.
201 Central Avenue South
Bethpage, NY 11714
(800) 453-3563
www.cole-and-son.com

FARROW & BALL
112 Mercer Street
New York, NY 10012
(212) 334-8330
www.farrow-ball.com

FINE PAINTS OF EUROPE
www.finepaintsofeurope.com

LES INDIENNES
1317 South Sixth Avenue,
Suite 139
Tucson, AZ 85713
(520) 881-8122
www.lesindiennes.com

MADELINE WEINRIB ATELIER
ABC Carpet & Home
888 Broadway, 6th floor
New York, NY 10003
(212) 473-3000 x3780

777 South Congress
Delray Beach, FL 33445
(561) 279-7777
www.madelineweinrib.com

MANUEL CANOVAS
Cowtan and Tout
979 Third Avenue
New York, NY 10022
(212) 753-4488
www.manuelcanovas.com

PIERRE FREY
979 Third Avenue, Suite 1611
New York, NY 10022
(212) 421-0534
www.pierrefrey.com

PRATT & LAMBERT
www.prattandlambert.com

RALPH LAUREN HOME
www.ralphlaurenhome.com

ROSEMARY HALLGARTEN
ALT for Living
110 Greene Street, Suite 411
New York, NY 10012
(212) 431-1000
www.rosemaryhallgarten.com

RUBIE GREEN
www.rubiegreen.com

THE RUG COMPANY
88 Wooster Street
New York, NY 10012

8202 Melrose Avenue
Los Angeles, CA 90046

4040 NE 2nd Avenue,
Suite 104
Miami, FL 33137
www.therugcompany.com

TIMOROUS BEASTIES
www.timorousbeasties.com

Lighting

CIRCA LIGHTING
www.circalighting.com

JUST SHADES
21 Spring Street
New York, NY 10012
(212) 966-2757
www.justshadesny.com

**Objects, Tabletop, and
Home Accessories**

CAFIERO SELECT
206 East 6th Street
New York, NY 10003
(212) 414-8821
www.cafieroselect.com

DARR
369 Atlantic Avenue
Brooklyn, NY 11217
www.shopdarr.com

DAVID HICKS
www.dh1970.com

DEYROLLE
46, rue du Bac
75007 Paris
33 (0) 1 42 22 30 07
www.deyrolle.fr

ERIE BASIN
388 Van Brunt Street
Brooklyn, NY 11231
(718) 554-6147
www.eriebasin.com

FREDERIC MECHICHE
4, rue de Thorigny
75003 Paris
33 (0) 1 42 78 78 28

GLOBAL TABLE
107–109 Sullivan Street
New York, NY 10012
(212) 431-5839
www.globaltable.com

HEATH CERAMICS
7525 Beverly Boulevard
Los Angeles, CA 90036
(323) 965-0800
www.heathceramics.com

ILSE CRAWFORD
www.studioilse.com

INDIA MAHDAVI
www.india-mahdavi.com

JAMALI GARDEN SUPPLIES
149 West 28th Street
New York, NY 10001
(212) 244-4025
www.jamaligarden.com

JOHN DERIAN
6 East 2nd Street
New York, NY 10003
(212) 677-3917
www.johnderian.com

MARCHÉ PAUL BERT
Paris flea market
Saint Ouen
Subway stop: Porte de Clignancourt

MICHELE VARIAN
35 Crosby Street
New York, NY 10013
(212) 226-1076
www.michelevarian.com

MOSS
150 Greene Street
New York, NY 10012
(212) 204-7100

8444 Melrose Avenue
Los Angeles, CA 90069
(323) 866-5260
www.mossonline.com

NICK OLSEN
www.nickolsenstyle.blogspot.com

PAULA RUBENSTEIN
65 Prince Street
New York, NY 10012
(212) 966-8954

PEARL RIVER
477 Broadway
New York, NY 10013
(800) 878-2446
www.pearlriver.com

PUCE DE VANVES, PARIS
Paris flea market
Porte de Vanves
Subway stop: Porte de Vanves

SENTOU GALLERIE
26, boulevard Raspail
75007 Paris
33 (0) 1 45 49 00 05
www.sentou.fr

TED MUEHLING
27 Howard Sreet
New York, NY 10013
(212) 431-3825
www.tedmuehling.com

TOM DELAVAN DESIGN
www.tomdelavan.com

UGLY LUGGAGE
214 Bedford Avenue
Brooklyn, NY 11211
(718) 384-0724
Design inspiration

**Inspirational
Places**

DONALD JUDD FOUNDATION
104 Highland Avenue South
Marfa, TX 79843
(432) 729-4406

101 Spring Street
New York, NY 10012
(212) 219-2747
www.juddfoundation.org

THE FRICK COLLECTION
1 East 70th Street
New York, NY 10021
(212) 288-0700
www.frick.org

THE MENIL COLLECTION
1515 Sul Ross Street
Houston, TX 77006
(713) 525-9400
www.menil.org

Where to Find It (cont.)

MUSEO NACIONAL DEL PRADO
Calle Ruiz de Alarcón 23
Madrid 28014
34 91 330 2800
www.muscodelprado.es

MUSÉE DE LA CHASSE ET DE LA
NATURE
60, rue des Archives
75003 Paris
(33) (0) 1 53 01 92 40
www.chassenature.org

MUSÉE D'ORSAY
62, rue de Lille
75007 Paris
33 (0) 1 40 49 48 14
www.musee-orsay.fr

MUSÉE JACQUEMART-ANDRÉ
158, boulevard Haussmann
75008 Paris
33 (0) 1 45 62 11 59
www.musee-jacquemart-andre.com

MUSÉE NATIONAL DES ARTS D'AFRIQUE
ET D'OCEANIE
293, avenue Daumesnil
75012 Paris
33 (0) 1 44 74 84 80
www.musee-afriqueoceanie.fr

MUSÉE RODIN
77, rue de Varenne
75007 Paris
33 (0) 1 44 18 61 10
www.musee-rodin.fr

Miscellaneous

HARRY
www.harry.com

JAK AND JIL
www.jakandjil.com

LADURÉE
21, rue Bonaparte
75006 Paris
33 (0) 1 44 07 64 87
www.laduree.fr

NOWNESS
www.nowness.com

THE SELBY
www.the selby.com

Index

A

African drums, 149
African wood pot, 159
album collections, 201
animal figurines, porcelain, 194
animal hides, 141
army blankets, 134, 141
artwork. *See also* paintings; photographs
    in bedroom, 182
    creating narrative with, 40
    in dining room, 67
    displaying, stylist's tips for, 28
    hung over bed, 110
    hung over sideboard, 65
    Indian maharaja portrait, 158
    inexpensive prints, 75
    kids' artwork, 64
    minimalist, 115
    mounting on walls, 28
    placed on floors, 42, 48, 102, 197, 221
    salon-style, 102
    tree-themed, 87

B

Bareti, Mauro, 143–51
barn, modernist, 35–42
bar setups, 243
bath linens, 104, 111, 162
bathrooms:
    adding funky feel to, 150
    atmospheric, 225
    brown, black, and gray, 111
    wall tiles in, 52, 104, 162
bathtubs, 162
bed linens:
    colorful, 52
    cotton percale and linen, 110
    from Ikea, 64
    simple and fresh, 220
    storage for, 161
    white Belgian natural linen, 63
bedrooms:
    with bare simplicity, 63
    with blue walls, 147
    bookshelves, 105
    brightly colored, 161
    dark gray, 182
    displaying collections in, 62
    Dorothy Draper–inspired, 52
    functional chic, 110
    guest rooms, 163
    with Italianate molding, 182
    kids' artwork for, 64
    with red hues, 19
    romantic, 220
    subdued, 104
    town house–style, 77
    tranquil, 95
    with woodstove, 163

beds:
    with dark birch headboards, 110
    with hand-painted frames, 147
    poster beds, 161
    with tuile-covered headboards, 19
bedside tables:
    chairs used as, 63
    homemade, 110
    personal objects on, 111, 139
    simple metal, 139
    vintage, 63
bedspreads, 104, 147
bench, lounging, 157
benches, wood, 162, 163
bike engines, 141
blankets, military, 134, 141
bookends, 113, 223, 234
books:
    art book collections, 77, 185, 195
    for creating cozy feeling, 193
    displaying as art objects, 65, 193
    stacked on floor, 16, 193
    stacked on tables, 75, 98, 193
bookshelves:
    bedroom, 105
    bench used as, 163
    built-in, 185
    custom, 98
    displaying objects on, 233
    graphic elements in, 55
    Ikea Lack, 113
    paintings placed around, 114
    tabletop objects on, 59
    used as room divider, 197
    wall-length, 193
bowls:
    café au lait, 63, 237
    ironstone, 209
    mixing, 155
    porcelain, 207
box collections, 55
boxes, for side tables, 51, 231
boxes, storage, 51
buffet tables, 100
bunny, inflatable Indian, 168

C

cabinets:
    built-in, 155
    "cabinet of curiosities," 211
    china cabinets, 108
    from Ikea, 19, 59
    from India, 157
    kitchen, 203, 207
    metal, 91, 207
    Paul McCobb wall cabinet, 48
    reclaimed, 144
candelabras, 139, 203
candlesticks, 115, 134, 241
carpeting, wall-to-wall, 51, 52

carpets, 149, 151
chairs:
    anemone, 124
    Billy Baldwin, 181
    blue tufted, 123
    Campana brothers, 124
    canvas cushions for, 61
    chrome, 167
    covered in cotton duck fabric, 113
    Eames, 102, 149
    Eames rocker, 61
    faux-antique, 203
    French bergère, 26
    Karim Rashid butterfly, 121
    leather, 126
    Louis XVI, 184, 197
    metal school chairs, 134
    midcentury-modern, 96
    1950s, 157, 167
    1940s French, 218
    Oly Design, 203
    Philippe Starck, 197
    placing sheepskin over, 96, 99
    plastic, 16, 73, 167
    reclaimed, 69, 149
    re-covered in silk velvet fabric, 26
    red, 103
    refinished cane, 69
    reinvented with velvet cushions, 69
    with rope seats, 203
    Selene, 16
    slipcovered, 113
    T.H. Robsjohn-Gibbings, 91
    used as bedside tables, 63
    vintage, 61, 224
    wrought-iron, 224
chandeliers, 121, 187, 193
chests:
    antique, 212
    antique-marble-topped, 163
    from Ikea, 64
    midcentury-modern, 136
china cabinets, 108
clocks, antique, 155
closets:
    for coats and shoes, 118
    creating, with drapes, 52
    with fashionable wardrobe, 127
    lack of, solution for, 147
clothing, 127, 137
coatracks, 147
coffee tables:
    as decorating challenge, 75
    metal, 195
    new-world style, 96
    placing trays on, 230
    reclaimed, 91, 98
    scrap-pile-chic, 98
    Willy Rizzo, 47
    wood-block, 141

coffer, wood, 168
color, 80–127
    black, 211
    black and white, 117–27, 133–41
    blues, 79
    bright, 95–105
    choosing, 96
    decorating impact of, 79–80, 96, 161
    grays, 79
    greens, 84
    neutrals, 96, 107–15, 161
    reds, 79
    as style inspiration, 16
    stylist's secrets for, 96
    white, 19, 57, 83–93
    yellows, 79
corkboards, 72
countertops, 108
cow head, Indian, 159
cupboards, 59
curtains, airy white, 141

D

dash of style touches, 226–47
    flowers, 245–47
    shelves, 233–38
    side tables, 229–31
    tabletops, 241–43
Dayton, Eva and Gentry, 133–41
Delevan, Tom, 179–88
desks, 16, 103, 198
dining areas:
    Danish modern, 67
    dark furniture in, 87
    with English garden theme, 21
    fashion-world sleek, 22
    small, 101
    with taupe and pink décor, 95
dining tables:
    banquet-like, 121
    cherrywood, 212
    designed by owner, 101
    Formica, 121
    French, 167
    Hans Wegner, 203
    by Tibor Kalman, 67
    used as worktable, 67
    X-base tables, 71, 73
drapes, 52, 181
drums, African, 149

F

fireplaces, 167, 182
floors. *See also* rugs
    black, 124
    checkered-tile, 225
    gray, 89
    green, 15
    honey-colored, 193
    light-colored, visual impact of, 113
    marble, 118
    wall-to-wall carpeting on, 51, 52
    white, 15, 188

flower light, 168
flowers:
    adding freshness with, 77, 115
    adding organic feel with, 84
    arranging, tips for, 247
    buying, 246
    for home office, 134
    for kitchens, 59
    for room corners, 169
    for small vases, 163
    style touches, 245–47
    for tall vases, 171
footstools, tufted, 52
foyers, 42
furniture. *See also* specific types
    choosing, for white spaces, 85
    dressing up, with accents, 47
    mixing and matching, 47

G

Gallagher, James, 57–67
gardens, 92–93, 209
glass vessels, displaying, 238
Goodman, Lauren, 45–55
Gray, Andy, 83–93

H

Hallgarten, Rosemary, 35–42
hallways, 118
headboards, for beds, 19, 110
home offices. *See* office spaces

I

Indian bunny, 168
Indian cow head, 159
Indian maharaja portrait, 158
inspiration, searching for, 11–12

J

Jones, Victoria, 69–77

K

kitchens:
    blue and yellow, 100
    country-style, 155
    displaying knickknacks in, 168
    French-style, 203
    galley, 187
    geometric patterns in, 100
    lighthearted touches for, 121
    minimalist, 108
    with old-world charm, 223
    personalizing, 72
    shelving in, 237
    small, 187, 207
    white, 59, 88–89
    yellow, 95
Kling, Cynthia and Phil, 153–63

L

lace, handmade, 150
lamps:
    for bedside table, 139
    bouillote, 187
    bright green, 161
    for corner spaces, 51
    desk lamps, for living room, 229
    flower light, 171
    glass, 172
    from Ikea, 64, 110
    industrial-style, 52
    Italian glass, 75
    Kartell ceiling lamp, 59
    mouth-blown-glass, 101
    silver, 113
    standing lamps, 73
    table lamps, choosing, 229
    table lamps, placed on floor, 99, 157
    white ribbon lamp, 229
leather boots, 144
library area, informal, 157
light fixtures. *See also* lamps
    Campbell's-soup-can, 121
    chandeliers, 121, 187, 193
    low-hanging, 104
    paper lanterns, 181
    sconces, 87, 182
linens, bath, 104, 111, 162
linens, bed:
    colorful, 52
    cotton percale and linen, 110
    from Ikea, 64
    simple and fresh, 220
    storage for, 161
    white Belgian natural linen, 63
linens, table, 208, 241
living rooms:
    black-and-white-themed, 141
    black floors in, 124
    blue and pink, 95
    cozy, 215
    flower-themed, 171
    kid-friendly, 61
    large and open, 157
    sliding doors in, 96
    spacious and den-like, 149
    Spartan décor in, 167
    techie, traditional, and mod, 123
    white, black and silver hues in, 113–15
loft homes:
    Brooklyn, 15–28, 191–203
    Chinatown, 107–15
    Tribeca, 117–27
    Upper East Side, 95–105
lounging bench, 157

M

magazines, 67, 173
Maret, Russell, 95–105
Martello, Michela, 143–51
matchbook collections, 98

military blankets, 134, 141
minimalist style, 40, 41, 108, 115, 193
mirrors:
    adding texture with, 48
    expanding space with, 71
    nineteenth-century, 163
    vintage, 111
modernist barn, 35–42
mood, 175–225
    creating, stylist's tips for, 193
    decorating impact of, 175–76
    English garden, 205–15
    laid-back, 217–25
    modern and welcoming,
        191–203
    tranquility, 179–88
Morris, Pam, 57–67
music equipment, 141
music systems, 123, 126

O

objects, 129–73
    black, white, and goth, 133–41
    collecting, stylist's tips for,
        147
    decorating impact of, 129–30
    displaying on bookshelves, 233
    displaying on trays, 230
    with Far East theme, 139, 194
    grouping together, 129, 147, 151
    travel artifacts, 143–51, 153–63
    vintage and bright eccentricities, 165–73
    work-related, displaying, 61, 62, 151, 212
office spaces:
    in bedroom corner, 188
    created from closet space,
        134
    decorative accessories in, 201
    displaying artwork in, 28
    kids' artwork in, 64
    red hues in, 103
    shelving in, 38
    white, 15, 16, 188

P

paintings:
    antique, 157
    in dining areas, 87
    as focal point, 211
    Hudson River School, 157, 163
    Indian-style, 144
    Mitchell Hoffmaster, 136
    nature-themed, 149
    neo-Warholian, 114
    watercolors, 150
paint palettes, as trays, 164
paints:
    custom, mixing, 83–84, 161
    mineral-based, 96
    oil-based, 96
Parisian apartment, 165–73
photographs:
    adding sentimental feel with, 98, 126, 233

on bedroom bookshelves, 105
    clustering in tight groups, 39
    family photos, 39, 98, 121, 126, 233
    on kitchen walls, 121
    on windowsills, 51
plants, 51, 92–93
plates and dishes, 237
porcelain animal figurines, 194
porcelain bowls, 207
porches, wraparound, 93
portrait of Indian maharaja, 158
pots:
    African wood, 159
    primitive metal, 40
pottery:
    Darwinesque, 159
    Etruscan, 39, 42
    French, 157
poufs, 16

R

Rautenberg, Véronique, 165–73
refrigerators, 100
Ritter, Alice and Paul, 191–203
room dividers:
    bookshelves used as, 197
    cheetah-print-covered, 22
    chintz, 21
    freestanding Plexi, 121
    stylist's tips for, 22
rugs:
    brown striped, 91
    dhurrie, 47
    English floral patterned, 96
    ethnic, 157
    Heriz carpets, 151
    from Marrakech, 223
    Tibetan carpets, 149
    white cowhide, 61

S

Sang A and Jaime, 117–27
sconces, 87, 182
screens:
    cheetah-print-covered, 22
    chintz, 21
    stylist's tips for, 22
shelves. *See also* bookshelves
    bookends for, 234
    grouping objects on, 234
    hutch or cabinet tops used as, 238
    Ikea Lack, 16, 108, 111, 187
    kitchen, 237
    pantry, 208
    steel, 38
    style touches, 233–38
    wine crates used as, 103
sideboards, 62, 65
side tables:
    boxes and trunks used as, 51, 231
    chrome, 47
    displaying books on, 65
    Eileen Gray, 194

lamps for, 229
    midcentury Knoll, 42
    Milo Baughman, 181
    placing trays on, 230
    plastic, 59
    rococo, 101
    Saarinen, 181
    with sentimental value, 167
    storage boxes used as, 51
    style touches, 229–31
    used for bar setup, 243
    X-base tables, 71
silverware, 88, 207, 241
skull and cross collections, 139
Smith, Nathalie, 107–15
sofas:
    accents for, 157
    choosing, 172
    covered with natural linen, 215
    Danish midcentury, 28
    de Sede, 41
    from Design Within Reach, 61, 193
    Dunbar/Wormley copy, 91
    George Smith, 47, 181
    from Ikea, 25
    with Italian design, 193
    leather, 28, 41, 141
    low-slung, 41, 215
    metallic silver pillow for, 47
    midcentury, 141
    modern design, 41
    Napoléon III, 218
    old-world style, 96
    Philippe Starck, 41
    placing rugs over sofa backs, 41
    plaid navy linen fabric for, 25
    quilted throws on, 149
    re-covering, 25
    shiny silver fabric for, 172
    white slipcovered, 113
    wool and leather, 41
staircases, 42
stereo systems, 123
stone wall, interior, 158
stools:
    Mies van der Rohe Barcelona, 141
    Philippe Starck, 34
    Victorian, 151
storage boxes, 51
stoves, vintage, 88

T

table linens, 208, 241
tables. *See also* bedside tables; coffee tables;
        dining tables; side tables
    buffet tables, 100
    from Ikea, 59
    sideboards, 62, 65
table settings, 241–43
tabletop objects, 59
tassels, decorating with, 26
Taylor, Lindsey, 205–15
texture, 31–77

texture (continued)
  in boxy apartment, 69–77
  decorating impact of, 31–32
  in modernist barn, 35–42
  in 1960s apartment, 45–55
  Scandinavian simplicity, 57–67
  visual, stylist's tips for, 47
tiles, floor, 225
tiles, wall, 52, 104, 162
toilet-paper holder, 150
trays, 164, 230
trunks:
  cut-wood, 65
  early-American, 161
  painted, 197
  used as side tables, 65, 231

V

vases:
  bud vase, 111
  chinoiserie, 96
  flea market, 147
  hand-painted, 173
  Harry Dean, 113
  jars or bottles used as, 21
  with nostalgic charm, 105
  round raku, 114
  tall, 171
  Ted Muehling, 123
  for windowsill, 123
  yellow, 157, 163
vignettes:
  creating from found objects, 173
  with personal objects, 62
  with photo props, 61, 62
  with seaside cottage theme, 215
  still life with blue vase, 211
  with traditional objects, 71
votive holders, 173

W

walls:
  blue, 28, 147
  dark, creating depth with, 223
  dark gray, 182
  mounting artwork on, 28
  mounting wall cabinet on, 48
  pale gray, 110
  powdery purple, 225
  red, 19
  slate gray, 103
  wallpaper, 52, 96, 104, 150
  whites and off-whites, 15, 102, 103, 191,
    193
  yellow, 98
windows, French, 169
windows, wall-to-wall, 193
window seats, 155
window treatments, 52, 141, 181
wine crates, 103
Wolff, Zoë, 217–25
wood coffer, 171
woodstoves, 163

Z

Zinto, John, 107–15